Light for the Journey

A Look at a Father's Favorite Bible Verses

Carl E. Creasman, Jr.

Published by:
Carl E. Creasman, Jr.
P.O. Box 217
Winter Park, FL 32790

www.carlcreasman.com

Printed in the United States of America

ISBN #: 978-0-9814638-7-2

For my daughters Logan, Meryn, and Brynn

I pray you drink deeply of God's gift of life, cherishing His Word to us as life-giving water. Giving you a foundation of faith is the best inheritance I could ever bestow upon you.

Table of Contents

Chapter 1

This book is for my daughters.

Back in 2005, when I was completing my book *Letters from the Front*, I wrote my final chapter of that book to daughters. I was clear in my reasoning: "I stand convinced that America is in peril and that peril has arisen as our country has walked away from God." I wanted them then, and now, to understand their role in the journey of a nation, and how to live as a godly person in a lifetime pursuit of His ways. In 2005, they were just children, my youngest daughter only five. Now, fifteen years later, they are all now young women. My prayer for them was that they "will be strong women of faith whose families will demand to participate in gatherings of believers supported by principles like the ones I've laid out in these pages." For that to happen, I decided to write this book of the most important Bible verses to impact my life.

This writing is also for anyone else who would read. Over the now 35 years of ministry, I've had the privilege to be a father figure to many. There are many to whom I would call my son or daughter in faith, knowing that we had had an interaction of spiritual dimension that changed their life. Others have told me of the role I played in their life from some leadership position that I held. It's a humbling thing to see others now approaching their early 40s realizing that I have been a significant person in their life. Each story speaks to me in my own journey; I know that I am still a human in process, learning to walk with more faith and grace every day.   Or, as Paul wrote, "I have not achieved yet" the goal of becoming like Jesus…. "but I press on."

So, where to start? Let me begin with this statement of truth about how I view the world:

I have been a Christian all of my life.

Oh, I understand theologically how that can't be accurate. The Christian faith is one that demands a conscious acceptance of the entire premise. That premise is a biggee, too:

- there is one God over all the earth, Who created all things;
- that the human used to be in relationship with God, but then the first humans broke the relationship dooming all subsequent humans to a fatal flaw, an original sin;
- that there is no possible way for the human to recreate perfect relationship with God regardless of their best effort because God is perfect, holy and will only accept similar holy perfection in His presence;
- but finally, that God did not leave us here in our fate but rather created a path back to Him….
- through an audacious plan that He would send a Redeemer who was really Himself in disguise….the God-Man Jesus of Nazareth;
- and that Being, fully God and fully Man, would actually have to die to provide the once-for-all sacrifice;
- but rather than staying dead like all other sacrifices, to display His power as God, Jesus would come back to life, fully resurrected;
- thus through the man Jesus, each human has the pathway to return to the relationship with God, both now in this world/moment and in the afterlife of eternity.

That is the story. And there's more after that, more about how we live after we make this claim of acceptance...but let's leave that alone for now. This set of conjoined ideas is what it means to be a Christian....to agree to that historical story. No baby can understand any of that. No little child can either, to be candid.

Still, I was blessed to be raised in a house where God had been supreme for years. My father was a Minister of the Gospel, as was his father and grandfather before him. We prayed and read a Bible verse before every meal. My sister and I spent almost all of our family's free time in church. There has never been a time in my life when I didn't know God or didn't believe in the Christian premise.

I make this point right here at the front of the book because you have to understand how central the Bible has been in my life. We would go to Sunday school, a small gathering on Sunday in order to study about God. We read the Bible at home and at church, and where I grew up, in my elementary school. In the summer, I would spend at least one week in Vacation Bible School....yet another concept of gathering children around the Bible where we would sing, play games, make crafts and yes, read the Bible.

At age 9, I started participating in Bible Drill where we would go back to church Sunday nights in order to read the Bible more. Think of a sort of spelling bee concept, with kids standing before adults, being asked questions about the Bible. Or, being tasked with either finding a specific book or verse from the Bible, or reciting a verse from the Bible. From memory. I can remember countless hours with our study guide at my home, memorizing the verses. I was never as good at it as my sister, but nonetheless from age nine to twelve, I spent even more hours with the Bible.

In July 1973, a month before my ninth birthday, I got my own Bible that wasn't a "little kid's" Bible. Or, so I thought...it was still a "Children's Bible." It was The Children's Living Bible, which meant is was much easier to read than the King James Bible normally used throughout our church. I devoured it. I read it completely through before I turned 10. Four years after that birthday, for Christmas 1978, at fourteen, I was given a study Bible, the kind of book that has copious notes that go along with the text. I read that through also, within a year or so.

Thus, before I could drive, I had spent every year of my life either having the Bible read to me or reading the Bible, memorizing and studying the Bible. All of those concepts about what Christianity meant was covered, stressed, explained and reviewed, over and over. Therefore, let me restate my bold proclamation.

I have been a Christian all of my life.

I realize this makes me sound "super holy"—and perhaps I was a teen who obeyed the rules more, did the right things and generally was an innocent relative the various temptations of life in the late 1970s—but my young life stood on a foundation of the Christian faith.

However, there is more to the story. As I left my East Tennessee hometown to go to Auburn University in 1982, I could not explain to you why the Bible was true, beyond just the formulaic "it's God's word." That probably was why at age 20, I had a crisis of faith where I questioned, for the first time, both the validity and the veracity of the Bible. Fortunately for me, through prayer and study over the following few years, God demonstrated to me in no uncertain terms the historical sturdiness of the Bible. While that story deserves more explanation, suffice it to say that I suddenly went much deeper in study and memorization, keeping God's Word in my mind and on my lips.

Through the decades of my adult life since College (now three decades completed since that graduation), I have spent more time in God's word. Over those years, new verses of importance have come to me. That's one beauty of the Bible...even after reading it through many times and studying it nearly every day of your life, there can be moments when you see a verse with fresh eyes. His revelation of truth continues even as one ages, and in those new years of older life, a verse can take on new significance.

Thus, if you really want to be successful, if you want to know how to live well and navigate in God's ways in the world, the Bible is the place to start. Over the coming pages, I want to not only show you my 31 favorite Bible verses, passages and concepts, but explain why each of these matter. The book will be laid out in a somewhat chronological way, in which I show you verses that were the earliest ones that really captured me, and then towards the end of the book share verses that God brought to me of importance later in life. You could read the entire book as a long story, or you could do a month-long study of the Bible through these verses, day by day, for 31 days.

These verses aren't, of course, the only ones to know. They aren't necessarily even on some list of most read or most memorized verses. Wonderful passages like John 3:16 or Psalm 23 aren't in my list, even though I commend them to you. These verses are the ones that God has made important in my life. These are the ones that touched me, guided me, admonished me, exhorted me at various and sundry times. I pray you find this useful. It's a Daddy's love letter to his children sharing key wisdom, for your best future.

Chapter 2

Isaiah 40:31—But they that wait upon the LORD shall renew their strength; they shall mount up with wings as eagles; they shall run, and not be weary; and they shall walk and not faint.

This is the first verse. I mean, it's the first verse that I can remember claiming. I'm not sure when I thought it, nor when I ever heard the term "life verse," but this has always been my verse. I had a picture of an eagle with this verse in my college dorm room. Over my college years, I was given keychains and plaques of this verse. It became my mantra, both before my crisis of faith and afterwards.

I know that I memorized other verses through my childhood. For Bible drill we would learn between 20-30 verses a year, and though some repeated, by the end of the three years, we had memorized about 50-60 verses. Sadly, I don't think I could necessarily quote them now, and certainly always struggled to hold onto "the address" of the verse (the actual verse notation), but deep in my soul those verses are a foundation of my Christian faith.

This verse, though, in College became "my verse" ...the first one I really would claim as my own. I was partially drawn to it because of the eagle. I've always loved eagles, and in 1982, I started my college years at Auburn University. If you know the school, then you know our battle cry cheer is a loud, long "war eagle." The words have a long-complicated history, and even the best Auburn historians confess that we don't know exactly where the cry came from. However, even though our mascot is a tiger, we also enjoy an eagle as part of our team. At Auburn, you could see three or four eagles in the special aviary on campus (now replaced by the Southeastern Raptor Rehabilitation Center).

I've always loved eagles, especially the idea of an eagle. My love was given a boost by my love of the United States. My family was a fairly typical one with a normal love for the country. Various family members had served in the armed forces, including my grandfather (before he became a Christian pastor) during World War 1 and my three oldest uncles who all served in World War 2. The nation's bicentennial came when I was 12, and though the nation was suffering a crisis of identity in the wake of Vietnam, Watergate, Stagflation and the Oil Embargo that raised tensions with the Middle East, I became a fervent lover of our national history. My parents took my sister and I on the proverbial East Coast vacation to visit the nation's capital, and on that trip, we made our way to Philadelphia, New York and the battlefield of Gettysburg, a trifecta of USA historical centerpieces. I loved our country, so I loved eagles.

I'm showing you the verse from the King James translation because that was how I learned it. There's a beautiful cadence to it with the four promises. As a young man looking ahead in life, each of the promises deepened my trust that regardless of what life threw at me, God would sustain me. Of course, this is not the only verse that makes such a promise, but what an important concept to grasp. Life is always hard, tricky, frustrating. People can make it worse, harder, more painful. It's so easy to get derailed. Easy to quit. Knowing that God is with you, not just with the idea of hopeful watching, but actively engaged in the next steps you choose to take.

- Renew strength.
- Mount with wings as in flight.
- Run without weariness
- Walk without fainting.

Each of these ideas shouts the urging to "keep going." Don't quit. Don't give up. When you feel like you can't take another step, He will give you the strength to keep going.

Even better, there's almost a sense of God giving you superpowers. You can fly. You can run all day. You can walk forever. When others finally give in, you are just getting started. In fact, like in some video game, you can get renewed strength.

It all depends, of course, on the first principle. There's a deal being made here, as there often is in the Bible. You do X, God provides Y. Here, it starts with setting one's life into God. I know, I know...that's not the words of the verse in the KJV. "They that wait upon the Lord...." The Hebrew word translated as wait by the KJV is qavah (kaw-vaw). The word can be also understood as "to expect" or "look for". Other translations will use the word "hope" or "trust," which is how the version I use most often, the New Living Translation, puts it—"But those who trust in the Lord will find new strength."

What does it mean to wait, to trust, to hope, to expect or to look for the Lord mean? I think there is an aspect of waiting as we typically use the word. There is the sense that we feel like something is coming, such as the start of a movie. I am in the theater, perhaps eating popcorn, maybe people watching or scanning a phone app...but I am waiting on something that I believe strongly will happen. Isaiah, who is the writer, is agreeing with that...that a wise person will consistently see their life in a constant state of waiting on the Lord, for His arrival. There is the feeling of the verse that links the initial action of the human with the four promises from the Lord...we are waiting in order to receive the upgrade strength.

Yet, there is more than that, which the other words like trust or hope or even "expect" suggest. The call is not to merely be waiting, not suggesting "be passive", but instead to be centering your life fully in Him. We need this promise of support because life is indeed exhausting. Life does take from you, and without some sort of deeper foundation, you will grow weary.

This notion becomes clearer by reading the entire chapter. Isaiah is one of the prophets of God, so you always know that he is writing in some context trying to urge his listener to either stop doing something ruinous or to be aware that God's patience has grown thin with judgment coming soon. With chapter 40, Isaiah has shifted from bringing the bad news of God's punishment due to the failures of "His people." From here through the end of his writings in chapter 66 there is a constant message of hope for any who will turn to (or back to) God. The first verse of chapter 40 points to this theme: "Comfort, comfort my people." That's God speaking to Isaiah. He doesn't want to bring pain, though He will in judgment over the failure of His people to live as He directs. He desires, though, to bring comfort like a loving parent who hugs their child after administering some form of punishment.

However, Isaiah has to go deeper than just a message of comfort. For many, when bad things come their way, instead of seeing God's hand in it, they wonder where God is. Perhaps God has abandoned us. Maybe He isn't even real. Or, if real, perhaps He is powerless. So, in verse 12, Isaiah begins to extol the greatness of our God. These verses echo what God says about himself to Job, starting in chapter 38 of that book. It's a beautiful display of rhetorical questions showing that God is unique.

> *Who else has held the oceans in his hand?*
> *Who has measured off the heavens with his*
> *fingers? Who else knows the weight of the*
> *earth or has weighed the mountains and hills on*
> *a scale? Who is able to advise the Spirit of*
> *the Lord? Who knows enough to give him*
> *advice or teach him? Has the Lord ever needed*
> *anyone's advice? Does he need instruction*
> *about what is good? Did someone teach him*
> *what is right or show him the path of justice?*

Isaiah is reminding his readers that God is WORTH trusting. In fact, he points out that there really isn't anyone else or anything else to trust. Why would you want to?

> *Haven't you heard? Don't you understand?*
> *Are you deaf to the words of God—*
> *the words he gave before the world began?*
> *Are you so ignorant? God sits above the circle of*
> *the earth. The people below seem like*
> *grasshoppers to him! He spreads out the*
> *heavens like a curtain and makes his tent from*
> *them. He judges the great people of the world*
> *and brings them all to nothing. They hardly get*
> *started, barely taking root, when he blows on*
> *them and they wither. The wind carries them off*
> *like chaff. "To whom will you compare me?*
> *Who is my equal?" asks the Holy One. Look up*

into the heavens. Who created all the stars? He brings them out like an army, one after another, calling each by its name. Because of his great power and incomparable strength, not a single one is missing.

The chapter rolls forward from here, rising in a great crescendo of how great is our God. Isaiah is perhaps shaking as he writes it down, trembling as the enthusiastic thoughts spill out. He brings it all to a powerful final question that would be on the mind of the reader. The previous 39 chapters have been one long condemning thunder of doom. What God is about to do isn't going to be pretty. You aren't going to like it. It will be painful.

In the midst of that pain, quite naturally, the person who had thought God was "my God" could be forgiven for asking whether God even sees the troubles? Others had asked the same question. Job certainly had. The people of Israel had while in slavery in Egypt. Hagar did. You remember that story, right? Read it in Genesis 16. Hagar was the servant of Abraham and Sarai. After agreeing to be a surrogate mother of sorts for the older couple, Hagar found herself being mistreated by Sarai. So, she fled rather than face Sarai's jealous rage. In the wilderness she ran, exhausted, with no hope. But God came looking for her.

See that? God came looking for Hagar, who wasn't even necessarily one of His "chosen people." God loves! He sent the Angel of the Lord to be with her, to strengthen her. The messenger announced, "the Lord has heard your cry." This is exactly what Isaiah is saying to the people, years later. My dear children, never believe that God isn't aware of your situation. Hagar decided, quite wisely, to call the Lord by the name "The God Who sees me."

The God Who sees you and me is aware of your situation. He isn't blind. He isn't deaf. He isn't weak.

> *O Jacob, how can you say the Lord does not see your troubles? O Israel, how can you say God ignores your rights? Have you never heard? Have you never understood? The Lord is the everlasting God, the Creator of all the earth. He never grows weak or weary. No one can measure the depths of his understanding.*

This brings us back to the central point of the verse. This is perhaps the other major reason I chose the verse as my life verse. Yes, the promise of renewed strength, even rising like an eagle was a core truth I wanted to maintain. However, the first part is the real hook for me, for how I wanted to process life. It was the call to be God's devoted friend. At that time in my life, as I surveyed both my life and the other Christians around me, it was clear that God wanted more than just Sunday attendance at some church. He wasn't asking just for some mere acceptance of those core ideas of the faith, but a deeper walk. Wasn't the entire first 39 chapters of Isaiah a testimony of this, that God's judgement was coming NOT due to caprice, but rather due to sad, constant choices by those who supposedly claimed His name intentionally not living out His ways?

Justice was gone in the land. Oppression was central. Those who should have been bringing the joyful message of redemption from a God who loved were instead distracted by living for themselves only. As I thought about my life going forward from this young age of 20, I wanted to be someone who devoted his entire life to God, to living with God and for God.

Do that, girls, and God will sustain you. Better, He will empower you. Choose to faithfully give God all of your life, all of the time.

Others, even the youthful and those young adults who feel so confident in themselves will become weak and tired, simply fall. But you...you who choose to trust, hope, expect and wait on the Lord....

He gives power to the weak and strength to the powerless. Even youths will become weak and tired, and young men will fall in exhaustion.
But those who trust in the Lord will find new strength.
They will soar high on wings like eagles.
They will run and not grow weary.
They will walk and not faint.

Chapter 3

Luke 9:23-25—And he said to them all, "If any man will come after me, let him deny himself, and take up his cross daily, and follow me."
(see also Matt 16:24-26; Mark 8:34-38)

If any verse has really captured my thoughts to guide me for most of my life, it's this one. I remember reading it early in life and wondering if Jesus really meant it. Did he really mean that we had to take up our cross? I decided that he did. And, from those early days forward, that was how I intended to live. Now, as I said earlier, it wasn't till I was about 20 that I became quite serious about this, but the echo of this verse has surrounded me since my childhood.

An aspect of that crisis of faith I experienced was that I suddenly realized the depths of this concept. I couldn't just randomly choose what I wanted in College, in some vain pursuit of money. If I wanted to be his disciple, I had to start with denial of my own ideas or thoughts.

This is much, much harder than we imagine. Or, maybe to say it another way, many people like to sidestep this to imply that Jesus wasn't seriously saying deny myself in actual or tangible ways. Of course, the thinking goes, "I can do whatever I want as long as I go to church, as long as I pray, as long as I state with my words that I believe in Jesus. If I say that I am a Christian, then I can pretty much do what I want and its good." For this view, the denial is simply the stating of purpose. Saying "I am a Christian" is all the denial required.

Wrong!

Such an idea is ridiculous if you do any study of all the things Jesus said. If you read the Bible, one overriding message comes through, and that is that your actions must line up with God's...and to do so will require sacrifice. This is the deny yourself part of this verse. Never forget that Jesus is always our model, so how did he do this? Clearly, throughout his three-year ministry, he shows us a constant position of denying the "whatever I want to do" concept. He expresses this clearly when he says, in John 5:19, "the Son can do nothing by himself. He does only what he sees the Father doing. Whatever the Father does, the Son also does."

Maybe the best example of how Jesus denied himself comes in the hours before the cross. Oh sure, the death on the cross itself is an example of that, but you can argue that at that point, the events of history were already rolling forward. Sure...as the all-powerful God, He could have just ended the agony sooner, even so far as to simply come down off the cross, whole and healthy. But as a human, we can see that once he is arrested, the actions are going to roll a certain way, not really different for Jesus than for anyone else. A mockery of a trial led by a group of powerful people who want to see him dead, willing to bribe any political leader necessary to get their way...kind of easy to see the way this is going to end up. But in the hours prior....

There, in the Garden, we can see the real choice before Him. Obviously, at that time of night, knowing that Judas is coming with the soldiers to arrest him, Jesus could have fled. He could have run. He could have chosen some other path forward. It was a real, true, serious choice before him. You have to remember that when we see Jesus making choices, being tested, he really is like any other human who has a choice. Will he choose whatever he wants, what he thinks is best for himself, or will he instead deny himself and only do what God calls for him to do? Here, in the garden, hours before a death he can easily see, he faces a true test of his determination.

And, for a minute, he begs God for another path. He does the same sort of negotiation many of us have done with God, looking for alternatives rather than the hard thing ahead. He is in agony over this issue, as Matthew reports in his gospel: "My soul is deeply grieved, even to the point of death." He asks his closest friends to watch with him, but even they fail him. As Matthew reports it, Jesus asked God twice for some other path, but concludes with obedience, with denial of himself. "Yet I want your will to be done, not mine."

That is denial.

The verse I am showing you, though, doesn't just ask for the one thing. Jesus gives three acts that we must undertake.

- Deny yourself.
- Take up the cross daily.
- Follow Jesus.

Of course, the three are linked through Jesus' example with the passion story of his death and resurrection. He denied himself. He took up his cross to his death. He was resurrected and walked forward, always going forward in life. For ourselves, I think it's like a three-cord rope, three distinct unique things twisted together to make one key thing. The life of the disciple of Jesus is this...a constant sense of denial while choosing death to self in an ongoing walk behind Jesus.

This idea of death isn't necessarily clear to modern people, but the cross was a well-known idea in his day. Perhaps if we said like this, with the second phrase being "sit in the electric chair daily" people would have a clearer concept. In case, though, you perhaps are thinking to take up your cross is merely another statement about sacrifice but not death, Jesus makes it clear in his next sentence.

He states a warning if you are confused about what he is asking.

> *For whoever wants to save his life will lose it, but whoever loses his life for my sake will save it.*

Again, the English words might hide the point from you. The word "save" in Greek more accurately means the concept of "rescue." You rescue things that are in peril. And, Jesus notes, if you are trying to rescue your life that is in peril, you won't make it.

Instead, he says, your choice will actual destroy that life. The idea of "lose" doesn't mean like "I lost my keys" but rather "the thing I wanted to keep is now fully and utterly destroyed." Of course, we do have this concept of loss... "she lost her life," but since our culture hates the idea of death, we avoid talking like this. Thus, many will approach this verse thinking maybe only of losing out on the best things or losing our way, and in doing so, deflect away from the cross.

As Dietrich Bonhoeffer said in his masterful *The Cost of Discipleship,* "Every call of Christ leads into death." I first read this in the months after my crisis of faith; Bonhoeffer was a German pastor who was martyred in the time of Adolf Hitler. My copy of his book in the early 80s translated this key sentence as, "When Christ calls a person, he bids him come and die." Bonhoeffer's point is that there is no discipleship, and therefore no Christianity, without this second aspect of Jesus' powerful statement. "Take up your cross daily." Without the idea of denial and death, there is no life. Bonhoeffer again: "Cheap grace is grace without discipleship, grace without the cross, grace without the living, incarnate Jesus Christ."

Jesus wants to make sure you are clear what He is saying. So, He takes makes it even more clear with his next sentence.

For what does it benefit a person if he gains the whole world but loses or forfeits himself?

See it? I think about this when I talk to my college students. Each and every one of them is in school with the idea of getting the proper preparation and credentials to go out into the adult world. They want to graduate at some point and get a good-paying job. If they are really candid about it, they want to be rich. Who doesn't, of course? They want to win the world. They want to find a future where there is never a worry about cash-flow, where they can buy themselves and their loved ones whatever they wish. Some of them will augment this desire for riches with fame too. Yet, in our current world, obsessed with likes and follows, where many have indeed gained some level of prominence through videos or social media, the pursuit of fame is intense.

My college students thus want to "gain the whole world." Jesus, in trying to be very clear about the deal He is offering, says that you might indeed gain the whole world, but the consequence will be that you lose yourself. You guessed it...the same Greek word is used there for "lose." Thus, Jesus is saying what does it benefit you to win the whole world but fully and utterly destroy yourself?

I know you would want a middle road, like "what if I only get well-off, and still am a good person and am nice...don't really choose death each day with the cross of Jesus but in general am decent....can't I avoid the destruction part"?   Jesus says no. He describes the journey through life as one of two paths, with the easiest one being actually the way to destruction. It is wide, smooth, level, easy to find and easy to complete...and it leads to ruin (see Matthew 7:14). That description by Jesus came fairly early in his ministry, when he gives a famous sermon recounted by both Luke and Matthew. Guess what word he uses to express the end result of the broad, easy way of life, of a life that gains the whole world? Yep, same word for "lose" (meaning destroy) as expressed in our verse here. God doesn't want total ruin for any of us. He wants to us to live with Him and for Him.

Now, look at the promise about living with Jesus. He flips the script. If one chooses their own way (thus, does NOT deny their self), in an attempt to rescue/save their life, they will instead destroy or lose that life. But, if instead this person will lose their life, they will actually rescue/save their life. How? Through Him.

whoever loses his life for my sake will save it.

For my sake...meaning "on account of me." The hint from Jesus is that socially, and perhaps physically, if you take the step to follow Him, rejection will come. This is why there is the initial word in the verse: IF. You can almost hear Jesus saying, "choose wisely."   And he does say that later in Luke 14:28 when he warns, "don't begin until you count the cost."   Don't begin what?   Well, in the previous verse he has restated the 9:23 verse, saying again "if you do not carry your own cross and follow me, you cannot be my disciple." So...make sure you want this. He gives two wonderful illustrations right after that about a builder and a national leader, showing how foolish that person would be if they started a task (building some structure or starting a war with another nation) without actually considering all of the costs involved.

So, we take up the cross...daily. Luke presses this point from Jesus. Mark nor Matthew includes this word, but Luke, who was with Paul for much of that apostle's ministry, understood that the journey of denial, of discipleship, is daily. The rejection for being a Christian or the sense of isolation from an unbelieving culture will come each and every day. Don't be shocked when this happens to you. Mentally you walk this road aware every day. Think as if each morning when you rise, you are picking up the cross before anything else. You are aware of His call that morning...."are you still with Me?" "Are you still going to be a Christian?" Follow His call to "come and die" that day too, just like the previous day?

Oh, but the reward is rich. A life lived fully in constant purpose, following Jesus in our daily life. We don't gain the world, but we don't see our life destroyed either. There are other rewards too, most notably heaven itself. To me, though, the point isn't some future heaven, but rather the awareness of having restored one's life to its original intent. Jesus describes that elsewhere as living life full, that he comes to provide life itself, and have it abundantly. Clearly, he doesn't mean abundant like the world would wish, as that loops back to the warning against trying to "gain the whole world" with money and fame and luxury. He must mean something deeper, perhaps even something mystical. We may talk more about that later, but for now I want you to simply see the offer for what it is.

For me, choosing to become a disciple of Jesus, what the world calls "accepting Christ" or "becoming a Christian," is the only path of life. All other options are false, leading to an eventual doom, an emptiness. Being His follower has provided me a deep purpose each and every day. My prayer for you is that you will also choose that same path.

Chapter 4

Joshua 1:9—This is my command—be strong and courageous! Do not be afraid or discouraged. For the LORD your God is with you wherever you go."

When we read that the journey as a disciple occurs on a narrow road (Matthew 7:14) and that the call is a call to come and die, that's daunting. Yes, we should speak like Peter did when Jesus challenged the disciples, asking if they were going to continue to follow Him now that they had seen the road was hard (John 6:61-67). Peter answers bravely, and perhaps with a slight wonderment at what it all would mean, saying "to whom would we go...you have the words of eternal life."

Are we left alone in our distress? Is God basically saying, like a tough coach, "suck it up"?

No!

Thankfully, God is with us. This truth is inherent in the full message of the faith. The road is not going to be easy, and our journey will demand sacrifice we just read about. In fact, as you will see through the remainder of this book of my favorite verses, the Luke 9:23 passage stands at the center. There is no way around that truth.

Yet, we are not alone! We are NOT alone...praise God. This faithful promise is throughout the Bible. Hopefully you remember from all of our Christmas celebrations that one of the names of Jesus is Immanuel. Matthew (see Matt 1:20-23) reports this story when he gives us Joseph's side of the story. Joseph was visited by the angel of God and told that Mary was going to have a baby conceived by the Holy Spirit, that his name would be Jesus, and that all of this was to fulfill the prophecy of Isaiah. In that prophecy, reported in Isaiah 7:14, we are told that the point is God coming to be with us, that Immanuel means "God is with us."

That is very good news indeed, and this same ethos was what Moses was telling Joshua as he commissioned the young man to become the new leader of God's people. In Deuteronomy 31:7, we are shown the historical moment when Moses speaks to Joshua to affirm his new leadership. He starts off with the important urging "be strong and courageous." Moses knew that the journey ahead would be difficult, which he explains in the rest of the chapters of that book.

Later, after Moses passed away, we are told that God spoke to Joshua directly. In this charge from God to Joshua, which you can read in the first chapter of the book named Joshua, God repeats those powerful words three more times (see vv 2-9).

>*Be strong and courageous.*

>*Be strong and very courageous.*

>*This is my command—be strong and courageous.*

As you may know, the call to courage or to not be afraid is repeated multiple times in the Bible. For instance, look at Psalm 31:23-24, where the writer proclaims "Love the Lord, all you godly ones! For the Lord protects those who are loyal to him, but he harshly punishes the arrogant. So be strong and courageous, all you who put your hope in the Lord!" As you girls are on your life journey, hold to those words.

I remember hearing sermons about this passage and memorizing this verse from Joshua when I was young. It's among the most familiar verses because God knows we are easily discouraged. We are easily dissuaded from the hard task, especially when it looks like we might face opposition. It's not that we are lazy necessarily, but that it's just hard. In those moments of a thing taxing us at the deepest levels, something inside wants to back off. It is just easier to find a different road.

Joshua had to have some of that same concern. He had faced challenging tasks before this moment, but now, he had the top level of responsibility. I remember leadership moments in my life, such as when I took over as the Head Age-Group Coach or was elected the President of the Valencia College Faculty Association. You feel the weight of leadership, aware that your every decision has some significance. Your choices will impact many others, and in the end, you won't be perfect in your actions. Of course, none of my roles are as monumental as what Joshua faced, but I think I understand why God was repeating Himself.

Clearly God wanted to make sure Joshua was aware that when things would get hard, to not give in to timidity or discouragement. Rather, God wanted Joshua to dig deeply into his memory to see that God was with him, thus be strong and courageous. That promise is extended to you and me.

The Sovereign God is with you wherever you go!

Of course, Joshua still had tasks to fulfill. Read the verses before this, where God gives the encouraging words twice before. See the list of things He wants Joshua to do? If you want a simple list of actions to undertake or things to do for your spiritual growth, this is a great place to start:

- Remember God's previous promises
- Obey all of God's instructions and commands
- Do not attempt to alter or slightly change them around
- Study the Bible which contains God's instructions
- Meditate on the Bible day and night
- Obey everything written in the Bible

As we shall see in some of the chapters to come, this roadmap of activities will be consistently stated. Thus, we can see that there is an expectation of God on Joshua, and on us. It's not like God is saying "I don't care what you do; I'll just hook you up." Jesus' words to us in the Luke 9 verse has already told us this. There is a deep semiotic relationship between the disciple and God above.

Jesus emphasizes this point in one of his most famous exchanges with the disciples. John again is the one who tells us about this in chapters 13-17. We'll look at a few verses from this section later, but if you go right to the middle in chapter 15, we get this beautiful picture from nature. Jesus says that He is the vine, the source of life, and we, the disciples, are branches that grow off from the vine. As we remain deeply connected, then we produce fruit.

We are told to remain in Him, and through that connection to Immanuel we will produce. The disciple is told to remain and also obey whatever God tells us. His words rise to a crescendo as he alerts the disciples that living like this will bring challenge and opposition, but the Holy Spirit was now going to come live with us. He tells us these things so that we will have courage in the midst of walking the narrow road.

Be Strong and Courageous!

Notice how God flips the exhortation to Joshua. First, he states it in the positive of being strong and having courage. Then, the very next line points out what it is not. It is not fear. Do not be afraid. It is also not dis-courage.

To be discouraged is a natural thing that happens to everyone. I don't think, though, that we often see it as the opposite of courage. Yet, that is what the "dis" means to the word. Previously you had courage, but now due to circumstances you no longer feel courageous. You are dis-couraged. That lack of courage halts our progress on the narrow road while we carry our cross.

God's words are designed to well up courage from within. Inside us, "EN" us...to be EN-couraged. When we think on God's promises, we can stand erect in the face of the challenges. We may not have the responsibilities of Joshua for an entire people, but the issues we face can still rob us of our courage. We become discouraged. So, God calls to us to remember that He is with us in order to bring up our courage from within, to be encouraged.

So, as we walk on the narrow road of a disciple, be strong and courageous. God is with you at all time, wherever you may go.

Chapter 5

Proverbs 3:5-6—Trust in the Lord with all your heart and lean not on your own understanding; in all your ways acknowledge Him, and He will make your paths straight.

I suppose in one sense I am giving you my overall lifelong journey with God. I will be listing all of these verses in a slightly chronological way from when God really brought them to my mind over my life. These verses from Proverbs makes the most sense knowing what I have told you about my journey. For all of my like until college, my walk with God was fairly simple. I loved Him. I went to church. I sang in the choir. I went on mission trips. I read the Bible. "Jesus loves me, this I know, for the Bible told me so." But then, as I wrote already, when I was heading into my Junior year, things changed. That crisis of faith moment brought me to a moment when I started asking questions about my life plans. I suddenly was deeply interested in knowing what God had in store for me, and that I was making choices that fit well in His plans...and equally didn't mess up anything.

So, in my childhood years, I was satisfied with just knowing that basic truth of faith...Jesus loves me. There wasn't really any need or thought about needing more. I didn't give much thought to my life as far as future ideas. I don't know if any of my peers did either. I wonder if you guys, as children of the late 1990s and 2000s, have had the same innocent processing? But then College came...first the decision of where to go and then what to do.

Auburn came easily to me. My sister, your Aunt Tina, had visited Auburn as a possibility for her studies, so when we went to the campus I was mesmerized. I was in the 8th grade, and thought it was the loveliest thing I had ever seen. It really was the loveliest village on the plains, and I knew then that was where I wanted to go. We visited again the summer of my Junior year, when I was still hoping to walk on as a swimmer, but even as that fell through due to my shoulder injury, I still knew I wanted to become an Auburn Tiger.

I mention all of that simply to let you know that until I came out of the spiritual challenge that I told you about in the first chapter, I had not really pressed into what God might have wanted to do with my life. I mean, I would say that "I had prayed about it," but not really. Then as a Junior, the dark night of the soul came. I was a History major. Yet, I wasn't majoring in that because I had some grand plan for my future. I certainly had no plans to be a professor or "Historian." Had you asked me, I would have told you that I probably would become a lawyer. I was thinking that maybe I could run for office someday, but mostly, I just knew one of the richest adults in my hometown was our lawyer. Not much holy thinking there, huh?

When I had gone to Auburn for orientation, they had a system then, in the summer of 1982, that freshmen would make their fall quarter schedule. Everyone who knew what they wanted to do went to those locations around the campus, and those who were undecided were left together, herded into a gigantic classroom. As we sat there, with our parents, I started looking in the catalog, and it became quickly aware to me that almost everyone was going to have to take the same core classes. Those general education courses would provide a foundation for every student. While there were some differences for students in engineering or the sciences like veterinary medicine, on the whole we all would take the same core classes.

I looked around at this massive crowd and concluded that I would have to wait hours to get my schedule. But, if I suddenly declared myself as a History major, then I could go to that floor and be seen by a specific advisor. I decided that, if nothing else, this would get me through registration quicker than waiting in this crowd.

Yep---my initial decision to become a History major was simply that I didn't want to wait around in the masses of undeclared students in that huge lecture hall. I did make sure that if I chose History that I could change it later if I wanted to. I didn't have anything else in mind, except maybe political science; when I found out that I had an escape plan...then I was off to the History Department to meet my advisor.

For two years, this was all fine. I liked it well enough, but if pressed, I had no idea what I was going to do. Then God intervened.

After that crisis of faith event transpired, I was heading into my junior year and for the first time, I really prayed deeply about what should be my next steps. I believed that I had heard God speak into my life about the future, but, as is typical for Him, in general broad terms. I knew my path it involved communication. I also believed it would involve other people. Beyond that, it wasn't necessarily clear. So, as I rolled into my Junior year, I started to ponder what my next steps should be. Ultimately, after prayer and reflection, combined with sensing God's direction through this verse, I added a second Major in Psychology, with a focus on human relation and behavior. I graduated with both a History and Psychology degree, exclusively because of God guiding my steps...a concept I really didn't know well till this verse and this moment.

My quest of discovery led me to these verses. I'm sure I'd seen them before, but in those days, this verse became, and has remained, a guiding mantra. Over the years, through my preaching and counseling, I have developed a robust concept of "knowing God's will for your life." Or, as it is often put, understanding "what God wants me to do." I will spare you most of that now, maybe to be added into another book later, so let's just consider these words.

This verse becomes like a math formula, though I urge to hold the idea of "formula" loosely. God is never put into a box of some human construct. Not only are we warned to not think we can give God advice, we are also told that we can't know what God is planning to do. Over and over again He says that the plan is beyond what you can even imagine....so, if you can't imagine it, then how in the world could you ever see it in some sort of plan to reject or accept?

But, God also is not trying to be coy or, as Gollum would say, "tricksy." He does want to us to not only do well in general terms, walking on a path of His preparing, but want us to accomplish things that He gives us to do.

It is the idea of "God has a plan for your life," a phrase used often (misleadingly, I believe) by many Christians, that causes concern. I mean, if He has a plan, then goodness knows I want to be correctly on the right path. God wants that too, and in these verses, He demonstrates how to get there.

Can you see the formula? There are three things we are asked to do. Then, and only then, He is on the hook for doing His part. This is important...we are not asked to do one of these three things. We aren't told that He will do His part independent of our three parts. It's a math formula. You need to add in all three concepts of your part in order to get to His part.

Trust God with our whole heart + Lean not to our own understanding + acknowledge Him in all of your ways.

The first part is perhaps the most obvious to grasp. Here we see the idea of choosing to be one of God's followers. The typical imagery of becoming a Christian is to "invite Jesus into your heart" or "trust in Jesus with your heart." There's more to this word "trust," but simply on the surface we get it. Trust God with all of our being.

This word trust is helpful as we examine it. In one sense, we are being told to lean into God as the One who will uphold us, much like we think of trusting a chair to hold us. We sit in a house trusting that the walls are going to keep the roof stable above our heads. This trust is typically so ingrained that we don't even think about it. Consider when, if ever, you approached a chair and then stopped to examine it to see if you really did think it would hold you? No...usually, we just sit. God is saying that we are to have that same blind faith in Him.

But trust as involving another being can also mean "to rely" on them. We trust someone in whom we feel confident that they will not betray us or that they will be there for us in a situation. I have had to be picked up at the airport, so I call one of a few close friends if your mother is not available, and when that person says they are coming, I trust in them. Note...I only call people that I DO trust, rather than just calling someone random or even a mere acquaintance.

I like the notion that the trust, in a physical way, is like leaning, especially when you consider the next part of the equation. God says to lean on me, and don't lean on your own understanding. This section is the toughest part of the equation. Taken out of context, then it sounds like "never use your own common sense or critical thinking." That can't be right because the Bible, in other places, urges the reader to pursue wisdom, using good sense, in thinking ahead and planning. We are encouraged to consider our strengths and weaknesses, the special giftings that God gives us. So, when we hear to NOT rely on our own understanding of things, we balk.

However, while the Bible does indeed say those things about planning, considering, and using wisdom, what God is doing here is pointing to a deeper thought. Remember, the point here is understanding how to know God's will, knowing direction or plans to undertake. At the center of that is the belief that God knows more than I know, otherwise why would I ask Him? So, we've just seen that the first part of this is to trust God broadly, with all of my being. The second part is something of a counterpoint saying that at the same time, in your trusting of God, know or remember that He knows more than you do.

Moreover, He knows the entire plan, the entire journey of your life. He is playing the game of life at a far deeper way. In the TV show Star Trek, you often saw the characters Spock and Kirk playing 3-D Chess, where the pieces could move between three distinct layers, as well as the normal horizontal plane. That's certainly a more challenging type of game since your pieces could be attacked from above or below. One move impacts any of the three levels.

God plays chess on 3000-D. His one move impacts a myriad of other storylines. He, and He alone, can keep all of that straight. So, we don't "lean not" because we, the human, are stupid or lacking, but rather because we know that He, the One God, is infinitely wiser than us.

Better, God operates on a different set of definitions. You saw this last time in the Luke verse...you gain the world and your life by dying. Seems pretty upside down to us, but God is actually saying that we do not fully understand the correct way of the world. In our broken state, and the world being broken as well, what we can comprehend is only partial truth, if that.

The apostle Paul reminds us of that in his many letters, but perhaps best in his first letter to the Corinthians. First he quotes Isaiah 29:14 writing "I [God] will destroy the wisdom of the wise, and I will thwart the cleverness of the intelligent." Then Paul lays out the conundrum if that is all true: "Where is the wise man? Where is the expert? Where is the debater of this age? Has God not made the wisdom of the world foolish?" We will look at this passage in more depth later, so for now just understand we lean not on our understanding because God's is on a different plane, a better and deeper perspective.

Thus, not only should we put more stock in God's depth than our own, that He knows far more than we, but at the same time, we don't trust our own understanding because God may be up to something that will seem unusual. He may be leading you to move to a city where you don't have any contacts. He may be asking you to sell most or all of your possessions in order to be better positioned to make a new move in life. He may ask you to turn down a promotion that offers more money so that you have more time to spend with your children or to start volunteering at a local food bank. He may tell you to take a new job that pays less money, in essence to take a step backwards, seemingly, but to do so in order for Him to position you into a new field or with new contacts from which He is going to use you differently.

The last part of the equation is to acknowledge Him in everything. This idea of "acknowledge" is also suggesting two things. The first is certainly the concept of recognition. Imagine you see a friend on the street, perhaps at the mall. To see that person and to call out to them is to acknowledge them. But what if, instead, you shrank back, perhaps duck into another store or hid from this person? That would be you NOT acknowledging them.

Pretty rude, you probably think…but what if there was something controversial about them? Imagine this person had recently been in the paper over some sort of charges at their workplace? Or, if you were at the mall with other work friends, and you knew the person you were with didn't like the other that you saw across the way. Would you acknowledge the other person?

God is saying that part three is, at least, openly admitting you are with Him. This concept is harder than it sounds. Sadly, there are many Christians who seem to blend in with the world to the point that it isn't clear they are on God's team. It is easy to acknowledge God when you are at church or surrounded by Church friends; what about at work? In your hobbies? This sense of acknowledging Him is an ongoing, daily activity. It is determining that you will wear His colors, let others know you are on His team, each and every day.

The other aspect of this third part comes within the Hebrew word typically shown as acknowledge. The root of it is knowing, so "to know God in all your ways". Here we see coming back to reliance or trust because of the mental conscious awareness of God and Who God is. I know who God is. I know Him, and in that knowing, in all of my life, I am conscious of His presence which then guides my actions.

The fun Christmas movie *Elf* gets at this very idea when Buddy the Elf, having moved to New York City and currently working Gimbels Department store, is alerted that Santa Claus will be coming to the store the next day. If you've seen the movie, you know what comes next.

"SANTA!!! Santa here? I KNOW HIM!!"

The wisdom writer in Proverbs is suggesting that is exactly how you should be thinking each and every day as you ponder your life. Part three of this equation is you, each and every day, with a hearty joyful exclamation, shouting "God? God here? I KNOW HIM!!"

So, that's our part, all three pieces of the equation...and to what end? Well, after that, when we do our part, God's part is that He will guide our steps.

A + B + C = He will make your paths straight

Or, literally in the Hebrew, God will make our path straight. This concept suggests God removing all obstacles in our way. God removing the hills and curves, dips and roadblocks. The path becomes straight.

You know I grew up in the mountains, and you know I love walking through them still. I find no greater joy than just wandering off into the hills, among the trees, with nary a path in sight. It is exhilarating to scramble up and down, often bouldering along the way. Stopping to determine direction and then getting surprised by an unexpected vista. However, as much fun as that is, there is also something equally thrilling to come out of the mountains, and finding yourself on a straight smooth, maybe even slightly downhill path to your car or house.

Note what God does NOT say. He doesn't say that if you do your three things that He will give you a roadmap or specific directions. Now, the King James Version does say "he will direct your paths." And that notion can be gleaned also from the Hebrew, but the "direct" part there is not in the same sense of "directions" that we typically would want.

We want God to give us marching orders so that we can say "okay, got it...I'll let you know if I need you later." Yes...there are a few times we see God doing that, perhaps most famously with Noah and Gideon. However, if you read carefully, those examples are the anomalies; most often God is saying "Trust me...keep walking." Or, as Moses experienced it, to simply have to follow the cloud of God by day and God's pillar of fire by night.

God is saying to you to trust Him and let Him direct you. You do your three parts and He will do His part. You simply have to learn to rely on this, that you won't often have clear, distinct directions. Yet, as you go forward, you can know you are in the right direction. I've heard the Hebrew expressed as if literally, God is placing your steps, placing your feet. You simply have to start walking. Just make sure you do your three steps first, and constantly.

If you want to dig deeper on this, then check these verses out:

i.   Other verses that support this claim: Proverbs 16:9, 20:24; Psalm 37:3-5, 23; Jeremiah 10:23; James 1:5; Ephesians 3:20; I Corinthians 2:9
ii. Verses encouraging the faith needed to believe this: Romans 8:24-25; Habakkuk 2:2-3; Psalm 33:18-22; Psalm 37:7, 34.

Chapter 6

Habakkuk 2:3—For the vision is yet for an appointed time, but at the end it shall speak, and not lie: though it tarry, wait for it; because it will surely come, it will not tarry.

I wonder how many people have bookmarked a verse from Habakkuk? I sure didn't when I was younger. That book, those writings from the prophet Habakkuk, was just one of those weird little books at the end of the Old Testament that were challenging to memorize. I realize now that part of my frustration with the minor prophets is that the Old Testament is not arranged chronologically. Yet, tucked away in this powerful short message of how God has plans that you can't understand nor tie to a specific moment, is this verse that captured my heart.

As I gained my spiritual footing after my crisis of faith, I was so eager for God. I started openly witnessing around Auburn's campus. I became a volunteer for my church's youth group, where I met my dear friend Scott Allen. I became involved with Campus Crusade for Christ and the Baptist Student Ministry. I read theology books by Josh McDowell, C.S. Lewis, Chuck Swindoll and Dietrich Bonhoeffer. I started teaching my own Bible study classes for my fraternity brothers. I had bought a

Strong's Concordance in an attempt to be able to read the New Testament in the original text.

I was confident that I had heard God calling me into a life of ministry, in service to Him. I didn't know how or what or where, but I was determined to follow Him dearly. I wanted my life to look like what is said about David from the Bible...that he was a friend of God. I had heard about how Billy Graham had responded to the question of "what could God do with someone wholly devoted to God." I wanted to be a Christ-follower like that.

Yet, as the months rolled by, nothing very spectacular happened. Of course, the fact that I was looking or expecting "spectacular" is a problem...perhaps something that all these years later I am still struggling with. However, I still assumed something related to obvious ministry would happen. It didn't.

As graduation approached, I wasn't sure what to do next. I was finishing with my History degree, but also with the Psychology degree. As I told you, in praying I felt God's leadership to use my extra elective hours to get another degree in psychology because I was going to be working with other humans. I wanted to get some training in the human mind and psyche. Yet, what to do next?

Because of my new devotion to God, heading to seminary seemed obvious enough, but as I prayed, I felt His hand against the door. Somehow, He was telling me "not now" for seminary. That made little sense to me because I knew that I needed deeper theological training. I wanted to be better prepared so I could fulfill this vision I felt that He had given me.

God had other plans, however, and so I simply followed as He directed me to stay at Auburn to complete my Master's degree in History. As I said in the last chapter, I had no plans to teach or work in a university or college, yet here I was for the next two years. I became something of a curiosity within the program because I was the one person getting the degree who would openly say that teaching was not part of any future plans. At that time, you could get just your Master's without pursuing a PhD, but everyone knew that if you wanted to teach in College, you would need the doctorate. Everyone in the program but me had clear plans to get their doctorate in order to teach.

I simply wanted to be on mission for God, and that meant out, active, speaking, serving...not in more college classes.

There I was in graduate school struggling with very challenging classes while also being a Teaching Assistant for our introductory world history courses. I can still remember grading 100s of multiple-choice tests for the lead professor wondering what in the world I was doing. This simply wasn't the plan as I understood it.

Now, let me pause the reflection to say that now, in 2020, I know God had called me, but that at that time I was fairly clueless to the concept that God's plans and my plans did not have to align. Even more, I was blind still to the point of following. That only He knows the way, and that His plans not only don't align but are often vastly different from mine. Living in the teaching of the Proverbs 3:5-6 passage was still new to me, and I was still a child to what it really meant to submit to His ways. I certainly did not "count" as being active in His ministry all the Christian activities I was doing. I was only thinking beyond College and, to be candid, in only what I had defined as "professional Christian ministry."

In those days, I would have simply told you that God gave me a vision to be one of His communicators, probably a speaker who traveled around, and I wanted it all to happen immediately. Sure, get whatever training was needed (seminary, most likely), but sitting grading freshman history exams was not a part of this plan. Reading historical journal articles about some aspect of French history or the English Civil war clearly was not helping me spiritually.

In that tension of my immaturity and lack of understanding, I began to get frustrated. Why wasn't God using me in the way that I believed He had said? Even in the face of all the Christian activity I was engaged with, in my mind, none of that was matching the vision. Then one day while in Graduate school, I stumbled upon this verse from Habakkuk.

The vision is yet for an appointed time.

It is for the future. It's not for now.

Wow. See, I was still lacking insight to how God measures time. We think in terms of minutes and hours, days and weeks. God never views the world like that. He can...but He does not typically do so. God simply is. He realizes that He is going to act within our time, though, so as He moves all the pieces in a far-reaching plan, unconcerned with days or years, He equally is clear that there is a specific time when He is going to act. When He does, as the human sees it, the event will happen on a specific time.

In that moment of reading, for my heart, God was assuring me that what I had heard from Him would take place. The time is appointed. I had never really thought about something happening in the future. This notion that I could rest in the knowledge that what He had told me could, perhaps, not happen until a future time was so helpful to me. The next phrase was equally encouraging.

The vision shall "not lie."

I like how the New Living Translation translates the Hebrew—the vision will be fulfilled. At the time Habakkuk had seen this vision, what he grasped seemed rather impossible. He was envisioning a time when the people of God living in Judah, including the city of Jerusalem, were going to be destroyed. It was devastating to him to understand this, and if you read the first chapter, Habakkuk is bold to tell God how disappointing this prophecy is. God, of course, doesn't care and won't change his plan simply because of Habakkuk's displeasure.

Yet, as chapter two begins, God shifts the vision to show what He was going to do to the nation of Babylon too. See, Habakkuk's complaint was that the instrument of God's judgement was the hated Babylonians. Habakkuk didn't think that was fair. Well, God shows again how He moves on many different levels all at once. Even as he planned to use the Babylonians for His purposes, He was also still planning to bring judgement upon the Babylonians too.

So, as Habakkuk says that "I will wait to see what the Lord says and how he will answer my complaint," God replies indicating that He moves on a different time schedule. His words to the prophet are that this vision, both of what is coming to the people of God and to the Babylonians, was going to be fulfilled. You can count on God.

To my ears, God was sharing a similarly confident encouragement. What He had shown me in a vision would indeed come to pass. Just not right now. That was a very encouraging point...and yet there was more. God didn't leave it there...and He doesn't leave you there either. We aren't told to just suck it up, but rather to have confidence in our God.

I don't know what you might be wrestling with in regards to a promise you believe God told you. Maybe it's something about your health or a type of job or something for your children.

Maybe it's a theological truth about peace or the return of Jesus. Whatever it is, God urges you to trust Him. The vision is coming.

"If it seems slow in coming, wait patiently, for it will surely take place. It will not be delayed."

Wait patiently. These two words are at the center of God's word.

Wait.

Patiently.

I didn't really know it then, but this is a central concept of walking with God. I had seen that word in my life verse where we are told "they that wait upon the LORD shall renew their strength." Yet, as I wrote in the first chapter, there the concept is more about placing your trust or devotion into God. Not really the point of waiting, like we have to wait for Christmas day to arrive. Here, God is really meaning wait, like in days and days, weeks and weeks, even years and years from now.

As I wrote earlier, God plays chess on 3000-D. He is moving the pieces, slowly, patiently, with purpose, but on His own schedule. There is no worry or rush in Him, and since He does not process time like we do, He has little concern about it all feels to us. For example, while Joseph was waiting years as a slave, God was simply choosing His next move for not only Joseph but for all of his family as well as for all of the Egyptians. For Esther, it may have seemed sudden to be thrust into a critical leadership role, but with God it was simply the next move He needed to make. Certainly, God knows of the years and the seasons, but He simply is unconcerned about them or if He needs to make that next move 30 years later.

I cannot stress enough how big this concept is in God's ways. I have spent 30+ years since He used this verse to calm me down, and now I tell you that waiting on God to move, to act, to roll out the plan is a central focus for the life of a disciple. He, and He alone, has the plan; you do not. You are to wait on Him.

We can wait with joy, with confidence, as Habakkuk is urged to do in this verse, or we can become bitter or frustrated. Note, I realize it's easy to say "don't get frustrated" about waiting, especially if you are in pain, in sadness. Waiting is hard to do, or at least it has been hard for me. I'm sure much of that is due to personal, private issues about my own walk with Him, but we know from the Bible that others struggled too. Learn to wait patiently on Him and His ways.

To help me, God has consistently taught me other verses on this exact same point. They tell the same story as the one from Habakkuk. Wait on God; He will come through; have hope because you know God is faithful. Check these out:

> *Lamentations 3:25-27—The Lord is good to those who depend on him, to those who search for him. So it is good to wait quietly for salvation from the Lord.*

> *Isaiah 49:8—This is what the Lord says: "At just the right time, I will respond to you. On the day of salvation, I will help you.*

> *Romans 8:24-25—We were given this hope when we were saved. If we already have something, we don't need to hope, but if we look forward to something we don't yet have, we must wait patiently and confidently.*

Romans 15:4b—And the Scriptures give us hope and encouragement as we wait patiently for God's promises to be fulfilled.

Hebrews 11:1—Faith is the confidence that what we hope for will actually happen; it gives us assurance about things we cannot see.

Psalm 33:20-22-- We put our hope in the Lord. He is our help and our shield. In him our hearts rejoice, for we trust in his holy name. Let your unfailing love surround us, Lord, for our hope is in you alone.

Do you see it my children? God will come through, but you must wait on His timing.

Chapter 7

Ephesians 3:14-21—When I think of all this, I fall to my knees and pray to the Father, from whom every family in heaven and on earth derives its name. I pray that from his glorious, unlimited resources he will empower you with inner strength through his Spirit. Then Christ will make his home in your hearts as you trust in him. Your roots will grow down into God's love and keep you strong. And may you have the power to understand, as all God's people should, how wide, how long, how high, and how deep his love is. May you experience the love of Christ, though it is too great to understand fully. Then you will be made complete with all the fullness of life and power that comes from God. Now all glory to God, who is able, through his mighty power at work within us, to accomplish infinitely more than we might ask or think. Glory to him in the church and in Christ Jesus through all generations forever and ever! Amen.

I believe it was as I was graduating from high school, way back in 1982. Or, perhaps it was during College, but it certainly came from my home church of First Baptist Athens. I still have it—a perfectly shaped red heart cut from construction paper. I think it was given to me in the context of a mission trip, one of the many that I went on as a young person through my church. I believe it came as a note of prayer and support as we were leaving, though perhaps it was in context of my graduation.

Ephesians 3:17-19.

That's what is written in the center of the red heart, in perfect handwriting [that's how you know it's not something I wrote since you know how poor my handwriting is]. In the King James Version, the Bible that I had in my youth, the words have this old English Shakespearean flow to them

That Christ may dwell in your hearts by faith; that ye, being rooted and grounded in love, may be able to comprehend with all saints what is the breadth, and length, and depth, and height; and to know the love of Christ, which passeth knowledge, that ye might be filled with all the fulness of God.

I remember finding the passage and reading after I was given the little red heart. I carefully underlined this part of Paul's prayer there in the third chapter of Ephesians in my study Bible. The person who gave this to me was saying it was a prayer for me, as I would go forward in life and ministry. The obvious core of the prayer is the notion that a follower of God is rooted firmly in love.

And yet, even as so rooted, you stand upon a foundation that is actually beyond your own knowing. The hope of the prayer tells us this, that perhaps, maybe, we could eventually comprehend just how big the love of Christ is. Wide. Long. High. Deep.

Maybe, the prayer hints, you might get a faint inkling of the immense size of love.

It's God's love that is at the core of the universe. In His love He determined to create the world, plant a garden and bring the humans into relationship with Himself. This isn't just passing love, a fondness for something. It's not friendship love. It's not erotic love. No, this is a deeper love. You may have heard this already, but in the Greek, there are different words that we translate into "love." Eros is the most famous, I think, because its connection to the romantic love idea. You can see that it is the foundation to our word erotic. Another word for love, in the Greek, is the word phileo. Can you see where the city Philadelphia gets its nickname? "The City of Brotherly Love." So, this is the feeling we have with friends, people who matter to us.

The third word used by the Greeks for love is the word agape. This is the word most typically used to indicate a higher, even supernatural love. I'm sure you can guess that many scholars have written many pages, books, articles explaining agape love (usually in comparison to eros love or phileo love). For now, I'll just leave you with the idea that agape is typically understood as deeply sacrificial love. It is a love that goes beyond just feelings towards another, but is an expression best understood by the sacrifice of Jesus. The famous John 3:16 passage says, "God so agaped the world that He gave His son." See it?

Paul is praying that we will begin to grasp all that agape implies, both in God's feeling toward us and in how we are to live as His disciple. Such a love is deep and wide, tall and long. Or, as King David says in Psalm 139, "I can never get away from your presence! If I go up to heaven, you are there; if I go down to the grave, you are there. If I ride the wings of the morning, if I dwell by the farthest oceans, even there your hand will guide me, and your strength will support me."

Paul wrote about the power and impact of God's love in almost all of his letters. To the Romans, he ends the powerful chapter 8, this way: "For I am convinced that neither death, nor life, nor angels, nor heavenly rulers, nor things that are present, nor things to come, nor powers, nor height, nor depth, nor anything else in creation will be able to separate us from the agape of God in Christ Jesus our Lord."

The prayer that Paul lifts up for the church at Ephesus is that we grasp this love. Frustratingly, just a phrase later, we see the reality that, in truth, this love passes human knowledge. The word in the Greek there means literally "to throw beyond." To throw beyond is to surpass all others, or qualitatively, to excel beyond. So, Paul prays for, well, the impossible--that we would know the love of Christ that surpasses, that goes beyond, all knowledge. In other words, "I pray you can know an unknowable truth."

What do we do with that, then? To start with, realize that you can't know this as you know a historical fact. This isn't knowing 2+2=4. Rather, Paul is pointing to something deeper, much like knowing a walk on the beach calms the soul. To experience God is to know him, and that is what Paul wants our lives firmly rooted and founded upon.

So, those were the verses on my little red heart that first brought my attention to Paul's prayer. Over the years, this letter to the church at Ephesus became one of my favorites to study from all the writings of Paul. I think I grew to like it the best because in this writing, Paul is presenting a primer on Christianity. Sort of like a freshman 101 class. The first three chapters present a basic overview of how to become saved, the mystery of God's plan for the humans. The last three chapters cover how such a Christian should live, both individually and in an awareness of being in a community of other believers. I have taught that if the book of Ephesians was the only book of the Bible that you read, you would be as prepared as possible to understand salvation (how to get it plus what is happening spiritually), and also what the next steps are to undertake as a Christian.

So, these verses at the end of chapter three are not just some random prayer, but a closing on the entire first section of the book. To grasp better what the prayer signifies those verses that were given to me as a young person, we need to back up a bit to the start of the prayer in verse 14. There, we can see Paul transitioning into the prayer and stating a key fact to never forget that all of life comes from God. God is the father of all things.

Then Paul makes his first request of the prayer:

I pray...he will empower you with inner strength through his Spirit.

Paul prays, asking God to empower each of us with an inner strength. Not knowledge like we might want, but Paul realizes that the deep love is, as stated, beyond our comprehension. To walk in that, we need an inner strength.

Then, see what comes next! That inner strength gives me the confidence to trust. Jesus then resides in my heart, he "makes his home" within me. He dwells me us; he comes to live with us not as a stranger, but like a friend choosing to live in your house. His presence helps then secure us with the ground in which to plant roots.

Paul prays that roots of my life grow down into God's love. Being rooted is crucial to sustaining. You ladies know that I have spent the last 10 years or so as a gardener. I love planting a variety of flowers and shrubs around our home. Sometimes, though, what I plant does not take root. What happens? Of course, the plant dies. I find it all quite mysterious, really; I really love gambling with a "cutting" from a healthy plant. This is where you take piece of the current plant and then put it back into the soil. The hope is that the cutting will eventually grow new roots in order to thrive where I planted it. Paul is showing us how to remain constant in the face of the various seasons of life.

With all of that—the empowering, Christ making a home in my heart, my roots growing deeply in God, and then walking into some sort of understanding of the richness of that love—is so we become complete with the fullness of life and power that comes from God. The fullness of God is a way of stating a complete experience of God

Yes and amen!

Now, skip down to verse 20 for perhaps my favorite part of this passage and the main reason I included it for you:

to accomplish infinitely more than we might ask or think.

Paul closes the prayer proclaiming truth about God. "Now to the One"....but look what Paul says. This One, our God, is able to accomplish, to do, more than you can ask or think. In the Greek, the word translated "think" is better expressed as "understand." Paul is pointing out that God is able to do more than you can even comprehend, more than you would even know to ask about. God moves and works beyond what you can imagine, as the NIV translates it. Beyond your hopes and dreams...because obviously if you can hope or dream it, then you can imagine in. God moves beyond that.

Do you see it? This is amazing. In fact, as it relates to God's interaction with us, I think this may be the most mysterious and incredible thing. Think back to the chapter on Proverbs 3:5-6. We noted that God makes our path straight. We are looking, in those verses, with a way to understand God's plan for our lives. And for most of us, we approach that with some concept in mind. It could be related to our own talents or something we find interesting. We think about if we should do this or that.

But here we see that God can do more than you can even imagine. You can't even pray for it, not really, other than just submitting to the mystery. When we say that God knows best for us, this verse hammers that point home. We can't even begin to fully know what is best to pray for because we can't even imagine what God can do. Wow!

So, we learn to wait in the tension, just like we saw in the verse from Habakkuk. I have often struggled with the space between what I thought my life would look like and how it has exactly turned out. When I get the most frustrated, I go back to this verse. Paul closes his prayer by calling out God's greatness, just as Jesus did in starting his more famous prayer. "Our Father who art in heaven, hallowed be your name." God the Father is greater than we are. All we, the creature, can do well is hallow, honor, proclaim reverence for and the holiness of this Great One. Paul's last sentence says it best: to this great One be glory in both the many Christians (the called-out ones) and in Christ Jesus, to and through all generations.

Now that is one good prayer!!

Chapter 8

Romans 12:1—I beseech you therefore, brethren, by the mercies of God, that ye present your bodies a living sacrifice, holy, acceptable unto God, which is your reasonable service.

Remember when I told you that I had spent years in Bible Drill? Well, this verse was one of the key verses we memorized. This is the King James Version, which is how I learned it and still know it. Stylistically, I think it is one of the most lyrical and beautiful verses like this; one of the times with the KJV really nails the verse.

At the core of this idea is sacrifice which, by the time I was in my mid-twenties, was becoming more clear to me. Now, to be certain, I was not necessarily happy with this. Much like the Luke 9:23 verse we've already looked at, there is nothing glorious to a young human to understand part of life's purpose (maybe ALL of life's purpose??) is to give your life away for others. That is certainly not what Americans were taught after World War 2.

So, though I knew the verse, it became more real with age. And what I saw was that God wasn't kidding. Paul wasn't trying to write with hyperbole. This really is what Jesus meant when he called people into following him. This idea is missed so often in modern Christianity, at least within the USA. The word "ease" or "comfort" is, sadly, the core concept in modern USA Christianity.

Yet, even with a casual reading of Jesus' life story, you see a repeated intensity that he applies to any who follow him. The "take up your cross" story quickly comes to mind, but look at other stories. Peter consistently gets the smack-down. He proclaims Jesus is the messiah, and gets praised, but then just a bit later, when Jesus says he is going to the cross to die, when Peter rebukes him, Jesus states "get behind me Satan." I mean, harsh. And then when Peter is the only disciple to bravely get out of the boat to walk on water, he doesn't get an "atta boy" for the effort. Instead, after he starts to sink due to fear, Jesus rescues him and then says that his lack of faith was the reason. John tells the story of Jesus interacting with his followers in chapter 6. In that chapter, Jesus confronts them about who He is and the cost involved. John writes "at this point many of his disciples turned away and deserted him." Jesus never goes after them or softens his position.

No...for Jesus, the path of the disciple is challenging and costly, and Paul reflects that here. There is, he states, only one reasonable choice for your life. It's the logical, intelligent, best option for how to live. Some translations suggest that this choice is an act of worship. It is that, certainly, but don't confuse this somehow with singing or Sunday-only choices. Instead, the point is a complete giving of your life in awe-filled service or devotion. Think of perhaps a slave, but not one there by force; instead, someone choosing to live their entire life as a slave of another out of love and devotion. If slavery is too controversial for you, then think about how a dog most often relates to the human owner. Unlike other pets (usually) the dog is slavishly (see, like a slave) devoted to their owner. Eager to be with them, eager to please them, waiting patiently for the owner to do whatever. That is the picture for anyone who is or wishes to be a disciple of Jesus.

Let's back up a bit, though. From chapter 8 through 11, Paul has been demonstrating the depth of the saving act of God for all people. Remember, Paul is a Jewish theologian. It is the Jewish people that God had picked as His special people through whom all of the earth were to be saved or receive a blessing. This idea of a chosen people had led some Jewish people to think in very exclusive terms. Paul however stresses that the opportunity to be brought into a right relationship with God, and through God, walk in harmony in the world was open to everyone. This is a magnificent truth, even if today most of that is obscure to many. Today, few understand or appreciate what Paul is stressing...that as non-Jews we previously had no access to the One True God. And yet now, through Jesus, we too can be saved.

It is in that spirit that Paul writes 11:33-36. Look at this proclamation of joy from Paul:

> *Oh, how great are God's riches and wisdom and knowledge! How impossible it is for us to understand his decisions and his ways! For who can know the Lord's thoughts? Who knows enough to give him advice? And who has given him so much that he needs to pay it back?*
> *For everything comes from him and exists by his power and is intended for his glory. All glory to him forever! Amen.*

Then, he writes the words we are examining: "I beg you, therefore" or as the New Living version has it, "And so, I plead with you." The Greek word is typically used in classical Greek texts in military writings as an exhortation to soldiers. It is a statement expressing how much you owe God. You previously had no access to God. There was no hope. As Paul said in verse 30, we were "rebels against God." We were at war with God, whether anyone wants to admit it or not. Now, though, the door is open to you if you will simply accept Jesus' offer.

Accepting, though, is only part of the story. If you wish to be his disciple, then there are next steps on the journey as we saw when we looked at the verse from Luke. So, Paul begs or pleads or beseeches you to do something...to place your body on the altar for a sacrifice. The sacrifice is to be living and holy. "A living sacrifice" would suggest that this is not in some future state of your death, or at the end of your life. Every day, at every moment, you are placing your body into his service, as a sacrifice. The sense is a constant state of "not my will, but yours God." To lay down as a sacrifice, of course, points to how animals were used in religious ceremonies. This is not something modern people are familiar with or will like, especially since for many, they value the life of animals more than they do humans. Just understand that in the ancient world, even in some cultures into more recent centuries, an animal would be killed as part of a religious ceremony.

If the animal is killed as a sacrifice, it does not get to live how it wishes beyond this moment. That is what Paul is calling us to see. You are to lay down your wishes or demands and instead be a sacrifice. Again, the linkage between this verse and what Jesus said about taking up your cross, living to die in sacrifice, is obvious.

Not just a living sacrifice (you making this choice day by day, as you live each day), but a holy sacrifice. This is the most challenging aspect of the verse. Clearly, I am not holy. I don't live perfectly, as many witnesses can tell you. Neither was Paul, as he wrote about often. So, he isn't making an unfair statement here. He can't be calling something from us that is impossible.

Yet, he is pointing us towards an attitude of our actions. I don't want to get too sidetracked here right now, as there is a lot more to say about the idea of how we are to live holy when none of are actually holy. Many others have written about this and there are different theological positions that can be taken on this point. For now, I just want you to think that this call to holiness is pointing you towards a goal.

I don't mean "in some future day you will become holy." And I don't mean that you can sort of forget about this word, knowing you aren't holy, and that you can worry about it later. Instead, I think it's fair to note that the process of growing in Christ is an ongoing progression. There is a linear concept for the one who becomes a Christian. I am made right with God in that moment, and then I live intentionally each and every day being made right with God, over and over, increasing and increasing, going deeper, understanding more. My life IS holy, and yet is also BECOMING holy in a progression.

There is an intentionality here, both in the overall sense of "intentionally choose to be this sacrifice" and in the holiness concept. I choose God. I choose to walk in His ways. I choose to reject sin, as best as I can, allowing Him to teach me more, correct me when I err, and call me into an ever-deeper communion with Him. The way of the disciple is ever closer to the holy walk of Jesus, becoming like him.

This is vital, this stance of intentionality. Note what Paul says about it. This kind of sacrifice, living and holy, is well-pleasing to God. The KJV says "acceptable." That single Greek word suggests something important. There is an unacceptable position. You can see this in the story of Cain and Able. Many people know about these two brothers only because Cain commits the first murder when he kills his brother. What leads to this, though, is that Cain attempts to worship God, and his effort is unacceptable.

It's a hard thing, I know, to see this with modern eyes. To almost everyone, it looks like Cain got a raw deal. It's not like he was NOT worshipping God. He brought a worship offering, some of the crops that he had cultivated. And yet, God alone sets the rules and guidelines for worship. He says this to Cain, both as a warning and exhortation, that "You will be accepted if you do what is right," meaning the worship gift was not what God demanded.

We don't like this. We don't want to really think about being rejected by God. We stamp our foot and suggest that God owes us. That He must accept whatever we bring or do, especially when the issue isn't something we believe to be extreme. Most of us will admit error if the issue is murder or theft or betrayal of another. On some religious point, though, we scoff and wave it away, that no one, not even God, can really hold us to account on some aspect of how life is lived if the issue isn't harming anyone else.

God, however, has guidelines and expectations, just like he did in the Garden and for Cain. There is a stance of what He deems "unacceptable." Paul is thus saying to us to live life clearly aware that you have a reasonable service to give God. Look at the great gift, the offer He has provided you. There is a way out of death and destruction. In light of that, present your own body as a living and as a holy sacrifice. This is well-pleasing and acceptable to God. This is what He wants to see. This is the only way to live!

Chapter 9

Romans 12:2—And be not conformed to this world: but be ye transformed by the renewing of your mind, that ye may prove what is that good, and acceptable, and perfect, will of God.

With this second verse from Romans 12, we come to perhaps the most critical piece of information about how to live as a Christian. When we consider the last words of verse one, we see He expects something that is considered "reasonable service" or "acceptable." We noted that idea is aimed specifically about how I should live my life as a disciple. For most people, once they take the step past basic acceptance of Jesus, there quickly emerges the recognition that there's far more to the Christian life and living that previously assumed. Jesus tries to warn us of this, but at one level no one can adequately convey to you the life ahead.

I think the movie *The Matrix* does a good job of demonstrating this. In the movie, the hero Neo has been on a search to understand what the computer simulated power, known as the Matrix, was. He finds an older guide, a man named Morpheus, who then prepares to help Neo understand the truth of his world. In a very famous exchange in the movie, Morpheus tells Neo that no one can simply explain about this mystery.

Morpheus says, "Unfortunately, no one can be told what the Matrix is. You have to see it for yourself." He then offers Neo a chance to understand, but the knowing, the true grasp of where the truth lies comes only after accepting, after diving in. To a large degree, Christianity is like this.

Of course, God is not hiding anything in the sense of some evil or harsh secret. Jesus made it very clear that following Him will cost you everything. The main writers of the New Testament echo this reality, with the concept of suffering front and center. One of the great tragedies of Christianity in the latter 20th century has been that many speakers and teachers focus more on ideas that becoming a Christian will make your life easy or great. They take Jesus words of life as a Christian of "life abundant" and then spin that into a life of ease and wealth.

While there is "life abundant," Jesus has not hidden that His definitions of things like "life" and "abundant" are different from ours. We saw this in Luke 9:23. It is clear in the last chapter. Still, there is an aspect of walking as a disciple in which there is no way to tell you what life will be like as a Christian. "You have to see if for yourself." Morpheus adds to Neo that "all I'm offering is the truth, nothing more..."

Well, the truth for the Christian is that you discover you are in the midst of a war of sorts. You discover that the world has been occupied by an enemy power, and worse, you have actually contributed to the destruction. The war is fought on at least two fronts or perspectives. There is the struggle within the world and culture where an enemy leads a variety of forces that aim to constantly mar what God would wish for good. This enemy lies, betrays, confuses and seeks to kill and destroy. He is aided by the fact that world itself is broken and damaged, and thus there are things like disease and environmental tragedy that bring pain.

The other front of the war is the place where you have taken an active part. It's the war inside of ourselves. The Bible talks about this often using the term "the flesh." It's not necessarily a good term to use because such can lead to a belief that everything tangible is bad, and only spiritual things are good. That is not what the Bible means. Maybe the word attitude or perspective or mentality could be useful here. The New Living Version using the term "nature" as in "your sinful nature." You see the effects of the war here in betrayal, lust, anger, selfish ambition, quarreling, lies, dissention, and envy. It appears in choices you make such as getting drunk, verbally bullying another, sex outside of marriage, stealing from another, or telling your colleague you will do a certain thing while knowing that you never will. These feelings and actions are yours and yours alone. You perhaps could claim you were tempted to do or say a thing, pointing to the enemy of our God, but in the end, you made a choice to do this thing.

This is a real war that brings the opposite of peace. This is why Jesus said he came to bring peace, but not the peace that the world talks about. The world talks about peace as being the end of conflict between humans. God says that peace is brought to the world when each individual has accepted Jesus and stepped into the right relationship with God. Then, as each person moves closer to God, knowing more of His ways, a decrease of harsh interactions between humans will come to the world.

So, Jesus and His disciples spend a lot of time showing us how to live in this world that is fraught with this conflict. We are invited, by Jesus, to be part of His invasion force. He's already performed the D-Day act, and now we are the rescued who get to join the conflict. To be effective, then, we need to prepare to engage in both parts of the struggle. Here, Romans 12:2, Paul shows us where that second aspect of the war is really fought.

The mind, and how we think, is the central battleground of our individual internal war with that sin nature. I love how this flows. Paul has just ended the first verse, as we saw, with the stance that if we have taken the proper step of giving our lives as a living sacrifice, that this is well-pleasing and acceptable service to God, a near-act of worship. Then, knowing we don't physically die at this moment, that we will keep breathing even as we give our lives in sacrifice, Paul wants to alert us to the pressure from the enemy.

The allure is to conform to the world. Think about it like pressing clay or wet sand into a mold. You've taken one thing and formed it into another. The enemy, through the world's culture, does this to us. Or, another way to understand this Greek word would be to imagine taking one of your dolls from childhood and then posing it in some scenario. You might extend its arm or have the doll sitting. You can imagine that the doll has chosen to participate, but you have posed it into the scene. You have conformed it into what you want. The world does that; it pressures you to be posed into the scenario it wants for you.

It does this through lies and misdirection. You see this with cultural concepts like having sex whenever you want. Research shows over and over again that most people can feel the emotional pain of casual sex outside of marriage. Many young people who have had sex report deeply regretting it, and yet admit that they believed most everyone else is doing it too. Hollywood promotes this by suggesting that virginity is as rare as a unicorn, thus if you are still a virgin (especially if into your twenties), something is wrong with you.

This same pressure is applied with how we speak to each other, lying, gluttony, over-consumption of things. The hint over and over is "everyone is doing that." Social media can be the worst at this as we see feedback that suggests the clear choice of culture is to act a certain way...and yet upon reflection, it is obvious that what we see online is only from a few people. Moreover, research shows that people are careful in crafting what message they send through social media. I'm not saying that people are directly lying, though some may be, but that the pressure to conform is evident even here, leading people to shape carefully what they post.

How do we fight back against this? Well, Paul does not say we should start arguing with culture or attempt to win elections or try to ban pieces of our current culture. Instead, God points us to the key that lies within. To win the struggle against being conformed, we have to let Him transform our minds.

transformed by the renewing of your mind

Two keys here---our volitional will to choose AND the actual transformation. That word transform, in the Greek, will be actually familiar to you. The word is metamorphousthe; can you see it? We get our word metamorphosis from this root. You know that the journey of a caterpillar to a butterfly is explained by this word. One website on butterflies wrote "the old body parts of the caterpillar are undergoing a remarkable, transformation called 'metamorphosis,' to become the beautiful parts that make up the butterfly that will emerge."

This is what God is saying here. We are to change in our form, a transformation from what we were before to a new thing.

Now here, in the letter to Rome, Paul does not go into greater detail about how this transformation happens. He does, though, elsewhere. In his letter to the Ephesians, in the chapter after his prayer that we considered earlier, he writes that we should "let the Spirit renew your thoughts and attitudes." (Eph 4:23) To the church at Colossae, he writes "Since you have been raised to new life with Christ, set your sights on the realities of heaven, where Christ sits in the place of honor at God's right hand. Think about the things of heaven, not the things of earth." (Col 3:1-2). To the Philippians, he urges to "Fix your thoughts on what is true, and honorable, and right, and pure, and lovely, and admirable. Think about things that are excellent and worthy of praise." (Phil 4:8)

Do you see the active role you must take? God is not promising to magically change your mind. This transformation demands your own action, which is the first key that I stated above. Transformation of the mind starts when you engage your own will, a volitional choice to act. Of course, God is involved in what happens. The first step you should take is asking God to do the transforming. I relinquish my will to Him, knowing that He is eager to see me changed. Still, the second step I take is to be actively engaged in the daily task of managing my mind.

Martin Luther, the great reformer, is said to have stated that in regards to sin, especially in our mind, that "we can't stop the birds from flying over our heads, but we can stop them from nesting in our hair." Paul offered one more idea of what this looks like in his second letter to the church in Corinth.

He writes "For though we live as human beings, we do not wage war according to human standards, for the weapons of our warfare are not human weapons, but are made powerful by God for tearing down strongholds. We tear down arguments and every arrogant obstacle is raised up against the knowledge of God, and we take every thought captive to make it obey Christ." (II Cor 10:3-5). In the context of that letter, Paul is talking about verbal argument against false ideas and concepts of God. He is defending his own ministry as a disciple of God. But that last phrase, to me, links perfectly back to what he wrote the Romans.

We are to gain a transformed mind. How? By taking every thought captive. You are on actively on watch, like a guard before the throne room. Every thought that emerges, you take it captive. You scrutinize it. Take it before God to let Him speak to it. You compare it against His truth that is revealed in Scripture. You force each thought to become obedient to God. You demand your brain only think on the things of God, the holy, the pure.

The battle within the mind is the central stage in the life of a disciple. Look further then to see what happens when we submit to God's will for His transforming work...our lives become evidence of God's will. Tying back to the Proverbs 3 passage, by seeking this transformation, we grow deeper in our understanding. Our natural way of thinking will change as we are transformed, and with our new minds, we grasp His ways.

Chapter 10

Galatians 5:22-23—But the Holy Spirit produces this kind of fruit in our lives: love, joy, peace, patience, kindness, goodness, faithfulness, gentleness, and self-control. There is no law against these things!

The last two chapters where we dug into Romans chapter twelve have shown what the Christian life looks like. It's a choice of a life sacrifice tied to the realization that we are engaged with an inner struggle of the mind. We want to avoid being conformed or molded by the world but rather be transformed, experience a metamorphosis by the renewing of our mind. This idea of change, especially worked out in the mind, is central to the Christian teaching.

We are broken, separated from God. We long for wholeness and reunion with the Holy One. Even if a person can't articulate it in terms of Christianity, everyone I have ever talked with senses something is wrong, off, not right in the world, and often they sense it "in my life." They have a variety of things to blame, including religion in general and Christianity in specific, but they still sense something isn't right. This is the common sense of the human worldwide.

It is that feeling that has led for over 6000 years into various efforts by the humans to achieve wholeness. Yet, 6000+ years later we find the world still broken. All of our best efforts have not achieved what we would wish in regards to peace and goodness. We simply cannot find a way to overcome our own broken nature, what Christians call "original sin" or the "sin nature." It is in every one of us, including the best of us...the nicest person, the kindest person, the one we look to saying, "she is a good person." Even in that person is a brokenness that leads to some moral failures, even if only internal.

God, through Jesus, offers us a way out of the trap. All we have to do is receive this truth that Jesus came from God, as God, and in our submission to Him, find freedom. After that, as we have said, then there remain steps forward and those steps forward take on many forms. Partly as we noted, there is the submission to let God renew our mind, to transform us.

The verse shows us what that transformation looks like. The apostle Paul is again the writer, this time to a collection of churches in a region of Asia Minor (modern-day Turkey) called Galatia. This letter is one of the deeper theological works about what is exactly happening in the work of Jesus. In one sense, this is a more intense look at what Paul was covering in the first three chapters of Ephesians.

In chapter five of Galatians, he makes a transition to the end of this letter by turning to what life in Jesus looks...however with a specific focus on not being trapped with religious rules. In a powerful first verse in chapter 5, he says "so Christ has truly set you free. Now make sure you stay free, and don't get tied up again in slavery to the [religious] law." He repeats this idea twelve verses later saying "For you have been called to live in freedom, my brothers and sisters." Here, though, he offers a counter warning about what freedom does NOT mean.

See, on the one hand, there is a rejection of old religious rules that have little support in the Bible. Most of these rules are man-made, or at best, a reading of a cultural truth from the past that isn't really something God presses on everyone. And yet, on the other hand, Paul is very clear that this freedom is not a suggestion that we can pretend like there is no sin. Many people want to act like it doesn't matter what they do; their position is as long as it feels good to them, they can move forward as a "good Christian".

So, right after the "you have been called to live in freedom" Paul continues with "don't use your freedom to satisfy your sinful nature." In the Greek, this is that same word "flesh" that we saw previously in the last chapter on Romans 12:2. The war we are having internally is between what our natural selves wants versus what God's holiness calls us towards. Like I said, we can try all we wish to be "good," but something inside us simply fails to achieve this desire. Even a very good person, from our human perspective, makes mistakes. Again, this often internally, maybe in their feelings about another or in terms greed or envy or bitterness...perhaps never seen outwardly but still true nonetheless. Paul, then, is warning us to not believe that somehow we are perfect just because we have become a Christian.

The war still rages within us. So...then are we doomed? No! Thank goodness. He answers this in many of his writings. Reading the seventh and eighth chapters of the letter to Rome shows this. The last three chapters of Ephesians, in broad terms, covers this too. Here, in the letter to the Galatians, he tells us that the key is to "let the Holy Spirit guide your lives. Then you won't be doing what your sinful nature craves."

Jesus promised his disciples, when he was with them, that He was going to leave us a gift after He returned to heaven. This is the Holy Spirit, the third Person of the Trinity. While there is much to be said about the theology of the Trinity, for now just be confident that He is "God with us...constantly." God didn't just send Jesus to be our savior, and then bring him home leaving us with a casual "good luck living well."

In his last night with the disciples, Jesus said "I will ask the Father, and he will give you another Advocate, a Comforter, who will never leave you. He is the Holy Spirit, the Spirit of truth." Later, he explained further that this "Advocate (or Comforter), the Holy Spirit, will teach you all things as well as remind you of the things I [Jesus] told you."

Paul is therefore looping back to this reality that as Christians, the Holy Spirit is here to teach us how to walk in the midst of this constant struggle. That is the best news. In ourselves we cannot simply will ourselves to goodness, no matter how badly we want to do it. We need God's help to be transformed.

So, as Paul is writing this in the letter to the Galatians, he spends the next few verses laying out what this struggle in our flesh looks like, and then more revealing, all the many ways our sinful nature is manifested. It's a long, discouraging list in verses 19-21 of chapter 5. He thankfully doesn't leave it there.

Instead, he turns to the verse I want you to learn. This was another one of those verses that I memorized at a young age through Bible drill. I think there is value in locking this verse down in your memory. I pray it often over my life, as something of a request to God. Here, Paul gives us nine wonderful characteristics of a Christian life. It is not a minor list, and in many senses encapsulates the totality of what our lives should look like. Let's read it again:

> **But the Holy Spirit produces this kind of fruit in our lives: love, joy, peace, patience, kindness,**

goodness, faithfulness, gentleness, and self-control. There is no law against these things!

Notice that he calls it "fruit." Think about that for a second. The fruit tree has this fruit produced through no effort of its own. The apple tree doesn't have to strive and stress to see apples emerge. Of course, the tree is engaged in the work to a degree, but my point is that there is a power beyond the tree that is bringing forth the fruit. The same is true for us.

Years ago, I wrote a song called "With One Look." The opening lines goes like this:

> *Look into the starry night, see You smilin' back at me*
> *Don't understand why Your loving hand*
> *Gives. . . gifts for free*
>
> *Want to walk, with Your stride, love big, limit free*
> *See the world through Your eyes*
> *Show love, grace, purity—grow these fruit inside me.*

We cannot demand this fruit to emerge in our lives. It isn't "the fruit of your life...." Paul correctly calls is the "fruit of the Spirit." This is something God does inside us, for us. That should remind you what I said earlier, that we have to relent and submit to allow God to do this work. We need God to "grow these fruit inside me."

Do notice that the first fruit is love. And yes, the Greek word there is again agape, that sacrificial love I told you about in an earlier chapter. I don't know that it had to be first; it appears that in Paul's mind each fruit is equal in importance. Still, I think it's appropriate to place love first as it reflects God best. He loved first, and that love is a God-love of sacrifice, what He called each of us to do in return.

I appreciate that joy is on the list. Think about that in reflection of the call to sacrifice, to deny ourselves and take up our cross. If there is a bitterness or frustration over this, then something is wrong in our understanding. Joy should be easily seen in the Christian. So too are faithfulness and self-control, both of which are also central for that daily task of walking in sacrifice, carrying the cross. Also, both are central in the daily task of submitting to Him in allowing the transformation to continue.

Each of these nine fruit are core attributes of the life Jesus lived; we are called to become like Jesus. This gives us a target, a thing to both pray for and then, more narrowly, focus on specific areas where I need to develop. Perhaps I need to understand more what God means about peace? Or maybe I am not as gentle as I perceive, especially with other people. This list gives us guidance about the life-long transformation that must go on inside.

God gives us a few other lists like this in the Bible. Each is useful for us. Check out James 3:17-18. James describes "the fruit of wisdom" or maybe "the attributes of wisdom": pure, peaceable, gentle, accommodating, mercy, produces good outcomes (in others, in events, in decisions), impartial, and not hypocritical. Similarly to what Paul does in the Galatians passage in vv 19-21, James contrasts his list in vv 14-15: jealous which also contains bitterness, selfish, boastful and ultimately lies against the truth.

Last thing...do you see Paul's closing sentence? "There is no law against these things." This is the New Living Version which may not be as clear as necessary here. Sounds like "hey, these are good to do; there's certainly no law against it." That's not really what Paul is getting at.

The Greek says "against such things there is no law. He is looping back to where the chapter started in talking about "The Law." Remember, the Hebrew people, as the people of God, had the Law which was initially written by God in the time of Moses. In the centuries since, though, many extra regulations had risen up which were part of the man-made rules I mentioned earlier. These are the type of things that got Jesus into so much trouble when he would break one of "the laws," and those leaders responsible for keeping watch would call Him on it. You can read about these various interactions in the Gospel accounts. At each turn, Jesus keeps pressing to say that there is a deeper aspect of the law that God was intending when He first gave it, but that the people had lost sight of that.

Paul's focus then on being free of the law is both experiencing a rejection of those constraints (free from the law) but also that deeper aspect of the internal holiness God calls us to (not free to satisfy our sinful nature). So here, Paul is saying that these nine attributes, these fruit of the Holy Spirit, that these are not governed by the law that he says we are free from. Instead, they are the evidence of walking in that deeper path Jesus spoke of. These are not part of keeping some law, he is insisting, but these are what emerges in a person as they allow God the freedom to transform us. You will express these characteristics naturally, even beyond your own sense of choice. As you allow God the freedom to change you, these things will simply just become what you are known for.

Now that is a powerful truth right there!!

Chapter 11

Psalm 1:1-3—Blessed is the one who does not walk in the counsel of the wicked or stand in the way that sinners take, or sit in the company of mockers. Instead, whose delight is in the law of the Lord, and who meditates on His law day and night. That person is like a tree planted by streams of water, which yields its fruit in season and whose leaf does not wither— whatever they do prospers.

The Bible is full of wonderful imagery and poetry. Much of this is found in the songbook called Psalms. It can be hard, at times, to fully grasp what is being communicated through some of the pictures. These verses from the first psalm are not that way. In a beautiful, abundantly clear image, the Psalmist explains the fundamental core idea of walking in God's way.

As we have been learning, the Christian is one who recognizes the contest, the struggle between living however I want and living in God's ways. We talked about the choice of self-sacrifice. We've seen that the battle of living well happens first in the mind. We now understand that this issue is both a problem with the world while also an internal issue with our own sin nature. We know that the first step is to see that God, through Jesus, provides us a path to Him, but that after that decision, we have a daily choice to make regarding our actions. And through our life journey, the Holy Spirit will—if we submit to His ways—grow the core attributes of a transformed life within us.

This idea of letting go but also making choices can be a tricky thing to grasp. On the one hand, as I have said, we win by giving up, submitting. We move forward in life by admitting that we can't do it...we need God's help. We submit, allowing Him to go into the transformation process of making us into a new creation. As Paul wrote to the church in Philippi, we can be "confident of this, that he who began a good work in you will carry it on to completion until the day of Christ Jesus."

And yet, at the same time, every day brings options from first waking moment to last thought at night. That I submit to God, knowing that I must relinquish control so that He can perform the work of transforming, does not mean that I am no longer in charge of my actions. I never become a passive mass of cells with no free will.

Ah, even as I type this, I am confronted with the obvious tension of the word. God is a mystery. He is the Wholly Other. He is the one in whom we confront with the numinous feeling of awe and fear. I have told you many times this truth...God is fully beyond us. Were He not to come near, to become Immanuel (God with us), we simply could not know Him. We would be like the Jewish people in the wilderness when they begged Moses to meet God alone so that they would not have to endure the power of His voice. I can't explain why this tension exists, but it does, and the Christian must learn how to live within it. Don't try to reconcile it or explain it away.

The Psalmist shows us the way forward, the same thing Jesus said at the end of his ministry. Obey the law of God. Jesus said, "If you love me, you will obey my commandments...anyone who doesn't love me, does not obey my words." In verse three of this psalm, the writer points to the benefit of this choice in life, saying that the person is blessed who takes delight, great joy, in the law of God. Such a person will be like a tree planted by a river.

Now this image is the one I was saying is easy to grasp. As you know from watching me plant my flower gardens, water is critical for plants of all types. Even a tree needs water to survive. Trees have very deep roots, more than the flowers and bushes I plant, which allows them to survive dry times easier than smaller plants, yet, even trees can eventually die if they have no water. So, you can understand that if a tree was "planted by streams of water," this tree will be in good shape to confront any type of season.

That tree will never wither. Its leaves will be glossy and full, lush and green. The fruit of the tree, whether apples or peaches or nuts or "fruit" that is really only edible for animals will come in abundance. It will be a healthy, wholesome, useful tree. The Psalmist has linked, for us, the rooting concept we read earlier in Paul's prayer to the Ephesian church. There, the focus is on God's love, His ethos of existence; here, in Psalm 1, the focus is on God's law, His way of living. That way of living can be one of growth and health, but don't miss a crucial concept.

In the imagery, your future can be one of not withering as long as you find joy and pleasure in the law of the Lord. What does it mean to take delight? Think of something you love to do. Now, think about how you feel the moment before you get to do it? Say you love going to a theme park...what is your emotion the night before? In the drive to the place that morning? There is a joyful anticipation; you can't get there soon enough. Or, think about a favorite meal or special TV show...in the moments before you eat or turn on the TV, there is a lightness to your spirit as you "take delight" in this thing.

We perhaps most easily see this in a good friend or loved one. Each of you has now moved out of the house, and thus left high school friends behind. Think back to when you came home for the holidays and you made plans to see one of these friends. Your heart might have even raced a bit in joy thinking of reconnecting. Your mother and I certainly know this feeling when we know you are coming home. There is this feeling of great delight, joyful emotions constantly welling up inside us.

This joy is exactly what is being stated here. This isn't the only place in Psalms that stresses this feeling. Most famously, Psalm 119 describes this joy, over and over again there is this deep desire for God, as I will show you later in this book. This idea of joy or delight in the law was something that caught me by surprise when I studied the psalm deeply. As I wrote in my book *A Love Ode,* "I had approached this famous psalm [Psalm 119] as just a long list of God's laws....And Yet...The Psalmist spoke often of his deep desire for God's word....I am still blown away with the passion in the words."

I rejoice in Your word like one who discovers a great treasure.

Delight.

There's more, though, isn't there? Not just "take delight," as good as that is, but equally this person meditates on the law of God day and night. All the time, God's laws are in this person's mind. There's plenty written these days on "mindfulness." That's just a new way of describing an old concept of meditation. To focus one's mind in deep and concentrated thought about an idea, word or phrase. If anything, meditating on something is forcing the mind to this one thing, dwelling on it, letting the idea or phrase become locked into your mind for later usage during times of active mind-use, like at work or in relationships. There's almost a sense of burying the notion deep into your mind so that later, subconsciously, it is there as a guide to your choice of actions. The Hebrew word used here suggests the person quietly reciting, over and over, the law or idea. There is a seriousness, an intensity combining both the idea of study and reflection.

And all of that is done constantly. Day and night. Not randomly. Not only on Sundays. Not when I realize that I've not really read the Bible in a while. It is a practice, a discipline. This is perhaps a good place to remind you that the spiritual disciplines of Bible reading, Bible study and meditation (contemplation on the Bible or memorizing the Bible) are three distinct things. The first is what usually comes with what we will call a "quiet time." Typically, especially for young Christians, they are taught that the quiet time is a short period, often in the morning, where a person will read a short section of the Bible, maybe read from a devotional book, and pray. Other things can be done, but those three things comprise the typical plan.

Bible study is something where you approach the Bible in an academic way. You will take notes. You will investigate what the original words are in Greek or Hebrew. You will probably consult commentaries on the book or concept you are studying. More than anything, Bible study takes time. If Bible reading in a devotional moment usually is 5-10 minutes, with the entire quiet time for most people being less than 30 minutes, Bible study will take you at least 30 minutes to get started. I urge you all to spend time studying God's word. There are so many helps in this, books you can use or strategies that are useful. As you hopefully remember, your mother first introduced us to Inductive Bible study with Precept Ministries when you were young. The helpful focus from Precept is that anyone can study the Bible, and you can simply use the Bible alone to learn, rather than needing some special degree or special books.

Meditation is different altogether. It obviously involves the Bible, but as in a starting point for the time spent. You will want a verse to meditate on; this is what the Psalmist says. This person "meditates on [God's] law night and day." You find God's law in the Bible. You read a verse, maybe even just a phrase of a verse...or perhaps more than one verse like this passage from Psalm 1. Then, as I said above, you chew on it. You think about it. You dwell on it. You turn it over in your mind again and again, reciting it, pondering it. You aren't so much trying to "figure it out," but rather just letting it be.

The person who lets the word of the Lord mold and shape, transform them, will grow deeper in their faith understanding. In my experience, this person will become a better person. They will start to see the fruit of the Spirit blooming. And, they will see the other fruit that naturally comes from our sin nature diminishes. Go back and read Galatians 5:19-21 again. Those are the kinds of things that will fade away. As they do fade away, the desire to be around those "fruit" equally diminishes.

This idea of not wanting to be around these sins is where the psalm begins. Read that first verse again:

> ***Blessed is the one who does not walk in the counsel of the wicked or stand in the way that sinners take, or sit in the company of mockers.***

The three-part picture is easy to notice; obviously the writer is making a comment about life with these images. There is walking, then standing, and finally sitting. It is possible that the writer is simply providing three distinct images of a person hanging out with the wrong crowd. Those to avoid take on three different names too: the wicked, sinners and mockers.

This is, of course, good enough for what the pictures mean. If you are a Christian, going to claim God's name, then you don't do any of these three things. Another way to see the trilogy of ideas is as a progression of getting deeper and deeper into the sin-worldview of those who reject God. At first there might be casual association (walking) with those who reject God's way of living, but by the end you are taking a longer-term position (sitting) that could be seen as identifying with this worldview.

So, you are blessed, happy, gaining God's favor if you do not walk in the counsel of the wicked. The verb is talking about getting advice from someone. Note, the psalm doesn't say you can't or should not ever hear the advice of someone who isn't a Christian; you are blessed to not WALK IN that advice. Meaning, you can hear their advice; I certainly have over the years, and in many instances the advice was sound. Yet, on worldview, on the deeper aspects of how to think about life and life's issues, I do not seek the advice nor ever walk in the counsel of these people. Now, I know the word "wicked" throws you. Like you, I don't perceive most of my non-Christian friends as "wicked." God, however, sees the world differently than you or I. And, even if I perceive these people as nice or good, to reject God and His ways is to choose a non-holy life. At the root, this person has chosen to ignore, perhaps even openly hate, God's laws.

Secondly, you are blessed or joyful when you do not stand around with sinners. Clearly, the wicked of the previous verse were sinning, so it's possible that the writer was just wanting a different word to use here. It might be, though, thinking that this is a second level...previously it's just a person who has rejected God's word (thus, in God's parlance, wicked....I know, I know...in current-day America, wicked is far worse than sinner). Now, though, this previously wicked person has taken their singular actions into a life-long lifestyle. Sinning, living short of God's mark for how we should live, is just how this person is each and every day. There seems also to be a sense of their own enjoyment of the sinning, a desire to continue in this path or set of actions.

The Bible admits that living for our sinful nature can be fun, that there is some pleasure in some things that God says not to do. Many confuse this point, thinking that a sin would only be something harmful or hateful or unpleasurable. This thinking then would suggest only a twisted or warped person would engage in sin since it clearly must be harmful to another. But that idea, that sinful acts are something warped or easily seen as bad is incorrect.

While there are things done that are sinful that do indeed harm others, God's ideas for how we live relate deeper into our minds and attitudes. Many acts that are not God's way seem to be harmless. This is why Jesus warns us about how we think, that those thoughts are equally sinful in God's mind. So, Paul warns the churches in Galatia about this, reminding them that "Those who live only to satisfy their own sinful nature will harvest decay and death from that sinful nature." (Gal 6:8) The Psalmist is warning you to not take a stand with those who have already determined their way of life will be in opposition with God.

The third image to avoid is the mocking of God. Let's follow the movement described: first a person simply rejects God's ways. That is wicked, but in this symbolism, is the most likely to be redeemed. The second picture is of a lifestyle opposite to God. Now, we come to the worst of the three in that the person openly mocks God. Equally, you can see that the individual in the story has gone from that casual connection, merely walking along, to a deeper identification by sitting with the mockers. This person has gone to a meeting, an assembly of mockers.

Overarching, whether just three distinct yet related pictures or a three-part story, notice that the blessing is for one who does not do any of these things. Blessed is the person who does not walk, stand or sit with those who openly reject God. Remember, it's a lifestyle issue...not a uber-picky question of actual sitting or standing. Don't get lost in arguing with the metaphor. God is calling you to a way of living unique in the world, that life of sacrifice that allows Him to transform you. You won't get there by choosing to look like or deeply associate with those who reject God. Instead, put your mind to work on falling in love with God's law, to delight in it so much you constantly think about it.

End result? "Whatever this person does prospers." It is a powerful promise. I don't want to take more time here on this specific concept, but I do want to warn you to not overextend this idea. It's not a blank check from God on whatever. In the metaphor of the tree, however, we can see the point that this person, this one who avoids connecting to a lifestyle of rejecting God, instead choosing to focus night and day on Him, will be like that tree. You will not wither. Your fruit will bloom in its season. You will become more in tune, more connected with God's ways...and that is prospering. That is a promise to hang onto.

Chapter 12

Colossians 4:5-6—Live wisely among those who are not believers, and make the most of every opportunity. Let your conversation be gracious and attractive, so that you will know how to answer everyone.

To this point, I have largely been moving through these verses that I want you to know in a chronological way. The first verses were among the most important from my childhood or youth, and then the last four or five have been verses God made important to me in young adulthood. This verse, though, is one that God impressed upon me more recently. I spent part of late 2018 studying Colossians and this verse really struck me as vital. As we just looked last chapter at lifestyles of those who do not claim God, seen in Psalm 1, I thought this verse would be more appropriate for me to explain now.

We will never live in a setting in which the sinful nature is not present. I have had the privilege of working in a "Christian-only" environment, and you may remember that your mother and I met while part of a mission agency. We lived closely with just a small group of other Christians. The sin nature was there and active in each of those settings. Not only do you still interact with other people while shopping, eating out, buying gas, walking in the mall or everywhere else, the Christians you are with are still fighting against that sin nature. That is not to suggest something was wrong with those people or organizations; instead, they were quite normal staffed with regular people such as myself who will never fully be free of their sin nature (that "flesh" we've been talking about).

Throughout your life, you will have every opportunity to do the opposite of what the Psalmist said. You can decide to walk with the wicked or stand with the sinner or even sit down with the mocker. We live in a normal society that seems to grow more ambivalent to faith. I think I can even make a good argument that the country has become anti-Christian. Whether merely ambivalent or antagonistic to the faith, this is the normal place of the Christian...to live as an outsider whose views for the greater good of society will be viewed with suspicion or even with negativity. Remember, Jesus already told us that the way of faith is very challenging while the other way of living is a broad, easy path.

Our verse for this chapter comes from the apostle Paul's letter to the Christians in the city of Colossae. It was near to Ephesus, located in the western part of modern-day Turkey. The two letters seem similar, as if Paul wrote them at the same time in his life, so just like Ephesians, the letter of the Colossians is split between a discussion of theology and then functional information about how to live as a Christian. In the fourth chapter, Paul beings his message closing the book with this last thought about how to use our time in the context of living among those who do not believe.

Literally, in the Greek, the verse says, "In wisdom, walk about toward those outside [the faith], the time is bought specific [special] at the marketplace." Here we again run into the familiar imagery of "walking around," the metaphor of life being a journey, what we just addressed in Psalm One. This phrase is very commonly used to describe one's lifestyle or behavior.

Immediately, we can see that Paul is urging his readers to be wise in the conduct of life.

This warning is throughout the Bible. God wants us to be very aware that we are His representatives. We bear His name. You are wearing His team colors. As you parade around town, be certain that people will see you and recognize.

Now, this part of the verse is actually not the part that really caught my attention. I mean, it is vital—"Be wise! You are on display." As you will see in the next chapter, this comes up over and over again. We are walking among others who do not see the value in God's way of living. In today's world, there is also a sense among many non-believers that Christians are the problem in our society. They come to that conclusion based on personal experience, either what they have lived or observed through media of Christians acting in ways that seem ugly or unkind.

Now, that idea of how a Christian looks and what other perceive about it needs more depth. Sometimes what is decried as "hateful" simply is doing what God actually commanded, and yet is so opposite to the current culture. Thus, God's way stands out negatively. We should still do whatever God commands even though we know culture won't like it. However, many other times what Christians say and do are not God's ways; they are simply being mean or unkind. So, I probably need to give you more on this point....but for now, just realize that the people around you are not only watching, but many have had bad previous interactions so that they have very little patience for Christians.

This is exactly why Paul's words here are vital. You must operate in the world with wisdom and a watchfulness. Jesus warned his disciples on this point, as Matthew points out in 10:16. There, Jesus is talking to his followers about doing ministry. He said, "I am sending you out like sheep surrounded by wolves, so be wise as serpents and innocent as doves."

Be wise as serpents.... Another version uses the word "shrewd" in the place of wise. Other translations write be "wary" or "prudent" or "clever." The snake typically does not trumpet or roar, does not respond in an arrogant or cavalier way making its next move. Instead, the snake is constantly moving with stealth, contemplating, thinking about the next move. Similarly, we are to engage with the world in similar insight. Yet, this is not our behavior in order to avoid others or to try and pull a "fast one" over on the world. Both Jesus and Paul show us this. Jesus says to act or behave innocent. Paul talks about valuing each moment as precious. Just remain cautious, being aware of each action you undertake.

This idea, then, is the part that really grabbed my heart when I read it:

the time is bought precious

The English translation, simply saying "make the most of every opportunity," does not convey well the part that grabbed me. In the Greek, the phrasing is more direct—"the time is bought precious." Isn't that a lovely thought? Paul is reminding us that each moment, each second of time, is to be considered like a rare item, something to be eagerly bought, and once bought, protected. His use of the word "time" means broader than a single point in time, and yet also a time space filled with many opportunities. Your life consists of a variety of moments in which each is rare and precious.

Do you think about life like that? I confess that there are days when I barely notice that hours have gone by. I've had entire days when I got to the end of the day and could not describe how I had used the time. That is the opposite of seeing the time has been bought precious. Usually, though, I chose to engage purposefully in my "each moment." Walking with awareness through your life journey takes focus and energy, but it can be done. Paul, having linked this with the first phrase about being wise in how we engage life throughout our days, is showing us that the time given to us must be valued.

His image then is of a person constantly aware that every moment is a precious thing, dearly bought, and sought at a high value. That person never wastes this valuable moment any more than you would be casual with an expensive purchase. This possession, the time that Paul writes of, is protected.

Of course, it then flows into v. 6 which speaks of how to converse, how to interact with another, in those precious moments. The Greek phrase that I translated as "attractive" literally is of your speech having been seasoned with salt. The way Paul writes it reflects a common Greek figure of speech that was used to describe someone who was witty or clever (not in an evil or devious way), who was known for sparkling conversation. Everyone loves being around that person, sort of the life of a party, who makes everyone feel good in the midst of a rollicking discussion.

Jesus spoke a parable to this effect, a story to make a point. It is the famous "parable of the talents" that you can read in Matthew's Gospel. The Master gives three of his servants a specific amount of money (a "talent" is a unit of money that in today's money would be roughly $500,000-600,000), and he directs or suggests that they should use this wisely. Two of the servants do precisely that, doubling the money given to them by the Master. The third person, though, does not. He hides the money so as to not lose it. While that may seem like a safe play, it is clear that the Master expected each of the servants to use their talents for the greater good. He wanted them to make the most of the opportunity before them. He wanted them to consider this moment, the opportunity, as precious and priceless.

In the end, the Master condemns the third servant as wicked and lazy. He had been given something of high value, and yet he did not seek to at least invest it in a bank to get some interest. He simply hid it, like someone who doesn't take advantage of the time provided.

God wants us to value each second of each day. Each day provides multiple opportunities to answer others about our faith. Each day provides us chances to defend justice, protect or aid the weak, to provide comfort to another. Each day we can be someone who "loves my neighbor as myself." To not do so is to be like someone given a roll of $100 bills and yet pays no attention, letting these casually fall out of the pocket.

Thus, the final image of the two verses is of a wise Christian who is aware that every interaction is unique, every moment is precious, special and dearly bought...thus is alert to know how (and in some cases, "if") to answer or verbally interact with someone outside the faith.

This verse is wisdom for living in a time like now. The vast majority of people we interact with are "those who are not believers." Our words and actions need to NOT be arrogant, not act like our faith or values or morals are the majority cultural view....but rather, be gracious and wise and attractive, the right or proper response to everyone and in any situation.

Remember Proverbs 3:5-6? God is directing your path. He is placing moments in front of each of us. He is intentional. In those, He wants us to be ready so that "you will know how to answer everyone." He wants you to be mentally alert enough, filled with the Spirit and with the fruit of the Spirit growing in you so that your conversation will, quite naturally "be gracious and attractive." He wants you to be like that tree planted with its fruit ready to bloom in season...the season when the conversation happens. He partners with us to continue His work of saving others, and to do that, He chooses to use me and you...someone previously saved.

Isn't that just a glorious thought?

Chapter 13

Galatians 6:14—As for me, may I never boast about anything except the cross of our Lord Jesus Christ. Because of that cross, my interest in this world has been crucified, and the world's interest in me has also died.

The cross is the central aspect of the Christian message. I'm sure by now you've figured out that the verse from Luke's gospel about the cost of discipleship is going to keep coming up. Throughout life, you will face the constant challenge, the question for the believer, as to whether you will place your focus on Jesus or allow yourself to be conformed to what the world considers "normal life."

I was speaking with a lifelong friend about this just today. I was noting that the great challenge of Christianity is that there never is an end. Each day is a call to return again to God, to kneel and pray, to seek His face and live His ways. It really never gets easier, in the sense that I coast along with no challenges, no confrontation with testing or temptation. Instead, the daily question is will I spend this day living my life in a way that points others to Jesus or not?

The Apostle Paul gives us this chapter's verse as almost a throwaway line at the end of one of his most theologically deep writings to the churches in the region of Galatia. These were some of the very first churches that he had visited once he started taking missionary journeys alongside Barnabas. It was in these churches that one of the first debates about the faith emerged. Remember, Jesus didn't really give out specific instructions about how the church should be developed. Just love and unity, as you have heard me say so many times. Yet, there were fair questions that came up.

One of them was just how tightly this new understanding of the Jewish God was to be tied to the old rules about faith and life. Remember, Jesus himself said that He had not come to abolish the law, so it could fairly be assumed that everything the Jewish people had learned would still have to be obeyed. And yet, within Jesus' own teaching, there was also clearly some sort of break with the old, a new understanding of "the law." He said at the end that He was creating a new covenant with us and transformed the Passover meal into a new love feast celebrating His own life and resurrection.

Well, in the days after the disciples started reaching others, as non-Jews came to faith, the questions really emerged. Paul led the way to conclude that the old rules about foods and circumcision were not really to be enforced, that a person could be a faithful Christian in a sort of new freedom. Paul's friend, the physician Luke, gives us an account of the debate among the Christian leaders in his history book, *The Acts.* You can read about the meeting in Acts 15 and also here in Galatians, in chapter 2. This idea, though, faced opposition and here, in the writing to the Galatians, Paul addresses his critics. In the end, as elsewhere in the New Testament, Paul points to the truth that we are saved by grace, not through any other means...certainly not through keeping dietary rules.

He starts to conclude the letter with those stirring words about the fruit of the Spirit that we've already looked at. He says we have freedom in Christ, and that we live through the power of the Holy Spirit. He gives a few gentle instructions about how to deal with a believer who is struggling with a sin, and a call to not grow weary in doing well. Looks like the end of the letter...but then he grabs the writing utensil one more time to add a strong rebuke to anyone who is still demanding circumcision.

Really, what he is addressing is someone who is boasting about their personal holiness or their marks of devotion. How many mission trips, how many Bible verses memorized, how much fasting, how many Bibles owned or how many times read....all of these can become religious trappings that are merely ways to show off.

So, he writes this verse as a rebuke of those ideas. Instead, he says, I want to NEVER boast about anything except the cross of Jesus Christ. Wow. What do you boast about? I know I can boast about a lot of things, including you girls. I love to brag about you and your many talents. I love to boast about your mother. Paul is making a deep point about the faith and against religiosity. I don't think this is a statement to say that you can't boast about anything...but if you try to show off your faith, well, that is the wrong boasting.

Jesus taught us this in the Sermon on the Mount. Go read Matthew 6 where he says to not do your good deeds publicly or that our giving to the Lord should be done as if our left hand doesn't know what the right hand is doing. If we do a religious activity like fasting, no one should be able to tell; no long faces or exasperated sighs when others eat but you don't. And for sure, don't let your praying be like those who just babble on or your make a huge production of the entire thing.

Instead, boast only of the cross. Why? Well, in I Corinthians 15, Paul explains it all very well. Look at it here (vv12-15):

But tell me this—since we preach that Christ rose from the dead, why are some of you saying there will be no resurrection of the dead? For if there is no resurrection of the dead, then Christ has not been raised either. And if Christ has not been raised, then all our preaching is useless, and your faith is useless. And we apostles would all be lying about God—for we have said that God raised Christ from the grave. But that can't be true if there is no resurrection of the dead. And if there is no resurrection of the dead, then Christ has not been raised. And if Christ has not been raised, then your faith is useless and you are still guilty of your sins. In that case, all who have died believing in Christ are lost! And if our hope in Christ is only for this life, we are more to be pitied than anyone in the world. But in fact, Christ has been raised from the dead. He is the first of a great harvest of all who have died.

See it? The cross is the central issue of the story regarding Christianity. If that event didn't happen, then our "faith is useless" and "we are more to be pitied than anyone in the world." We are fools, in essence, if there was no cross or resurrection. Laugh away at our foolish beliefs. YET—Jesus has been raised from the dead!! He died on that Roman cross, but he rose again. We aren't to be pitied. The historical evidence is secure that there was a man named Jesus. He was put to death by the Romans, who were very good at this task. Three days he lay in a tomb...and then, boom, even though there was a stone rolled to block the entrance, and a guard of soldiers present, Jesus walked out of that grave.

Jesus is central to the journey. Knowing Him, knowing God as Savior, is at the core of the entire story of salvation. The prophet Jeremiah pointed to this same idea in his writing. Go read Jeremiah 9:23-24. There, God says that the wise should not boast in their wisdom. The powerful should not boast in their power nor the rich boast in their riches. Instead, we are to boast only that "they truly know me and understand that I am the LORD." God is the only One to bring justice and righteousness to the earth. That plan was culminated in Jesus' death and resurrection.

This is what Paul is thinking as he comes back to conclude the letter to the Galatians. He's thinking about these other people boasting about their religious trappings, and Paul instead thinks only about Jesus. That cross, he says, is the only thing worth boasting about, if there is to be any boasting at all. Then he goes further; don't miss this.

See, it's not just the boasting, but rather what happens to my interests due to that cross.

Because of that cross, my interest in this world has been crucified.

It is dead. Now, Paul is not saying that we are to no longer care about our neighbors, about their spiritual condition. Instead, he is pointing to the idea that our own pursuit of worldly things, possessions, fame, positions, honors...these things hold no interest. This is really where the rubber meets the road yet again. It's very easy for me to proclaim that I am a Christian. To boast in my faith. And yet, what does my life testify about me? Does it show me as someone content in my life or am I someone in a never-ending pursuit of something of the world that I believe will satisfy me?

Even more, look what he says next.

Because of that cross...the world's interest in me has also died.

This point may be the harder thing to swallow. So much of the world, especially these days with the constant pressure to be seen via social media and the Internet, eagerly wants to have the world's interest. I get it. I like to be liked too...in person and online. We want to produce things that others celebrate. It's nice to be honored, recognized, praised. And yet....

Jesus warned us that following Him would not lead to fame, but rather to derision and mocking. A life of following Jesus would actually produce division as others reject the call of the Father to holiness. Even within a family, a person who pursues Jesus and His ways can face rejection and persecution. In the end, if you truly are walking after God, the world will lose interest in you. The more traditional rendering of the Greek here perhaps is more stark: Through that cross, the world have been crucified (killed) to me...and I to the world.

Take up my own cross. The call of Christ is the call to come and die. If I die, then I die to the world, its allures and false promises. And the world sees me as dead. The world has no more interest in me or my dreams and what I could become in it. My focus on the cross means that I am of no use to the world in the world's designs.

This verse has become quite important to me. I think you girls know that I have been driven by a zeal for God that has, at times, drifted over into a passion for my own success. Or, that I don't feel successful, so I then doubt my usefulness which then leads me to be more concerned about my success....a vicious cycle. As you know, in the fall of 2019, I believed that God had asked me to run for public office in Winter Park. I didn't win the election.

That kind of stepping out into the public sphere, even more than I previously had, really put this verse to the challenge. In our world today, if I really want to get elected, I need to downplay my faith, especially the more intense side of boasting in the cross. And yet, what I believe about our country, and thus about my city, is that where we have gone astray is in departing from the foundational aspects of our faith. Not that I think everyone in the country must become a Christian (though I would wish that), but that instead our system of government (one where individuals work together to achieve something) is dependent upon a mutual sense of morality and virtues. Or, as John Adams put it, we need both knowledge and virtue in order to preserve our liberty. For President Adams, that means a focus on education and on Christian morality.

For me to say that openly is to boast in the cross...and rush headlong into the point that the world's interest in me has died. Follow Him is a call to come and die...and yet live. We live even though we may not get elected, we may not hear the world's applause. But to die is gain, and in dying, we point others to the cross through our boasting only in Him.

Chapter 14

Philippians 3:12-14—I don't mean to say that I have already achieved these things or that I have already reached perfection. But I press on to possess that perfection for which Christ Jesus first possessed me. No, dear brothers and sisters, I have not achieved it, but I focus on this one thing: Forgetting the past and looking forward to what lies ahead, I press on to reach the end of the race and receive the heavenly prize for which God, through Christ Jesus, is calling us.

In 1988, your mother and I were serving on the domestic mission team where we met, performing the evangelistic drama *The Greatest Star of All.* As the team travelled around the country, we would perform in churches, and on almost every Sunday while travelling, we would attend a church. Early in our time performing, we visited a church in Alabama, and the pastor's sermon centered on this passage in Philippians.

I think I fell in love with this book, as you will see in subsequent passages, at this time. This is one of Paul's latter letters, and like Ephesians, could be something of a "how to" book on living like a Christian. Here in Chapter three, Paul lays out what became my defining method of understanding life, of what happens to us over time. At the time of the sermon, I was 24 and so of course knew little about life; now in my 50s, I see even better how this teaching should be central in your life.

The verses, as you can read, are a focus on how to understand what has happened to you in your life over time. More deeply, they are a statement about your own progress in discipleship, in becoming like Jesus. The sermon, and Paul's focus here in chapter 3, beings at the start of the chapter. And, as the pastor explained, we can see Paul talking about his past, his present and his future, and through that, how we should live each day….where our focus should be.

Look at verse 7—"I once thought these things were valuable." What things? Well, he's just written, in the previous verses, that he among all Jewish believers could make a claim for spiritual greatness. He's making this sort of statement because he is confronting other supposed Christians who are presenting different rules, different ideas for how to live as a Christian. Paul has had to challenge these people throughout most of his ministry; reading his other letters will make this clear as we saw in the previous chapter. It's almost like these people specifically followed Paul around, and then after he would leave a city, would roll in to undermine the work Paul just did. Part of their method was to talk big about their own talents and spiritual depth, and at the same time, tear Paul down. So, as he does in his second letter to Corinth, Paul is saying "if anyone has an awesome resume, it's me."

Yet, surprisingly, he says all that past success is worthless. He considers it worthless, pure junk. We can also see with the last part of verse 13, that even if you think your past was bad…we don't dwell on that. Nothing in your past is the final triumphant success and nothing is the complete utter failure of life.

In verse 8, Paul continues this statement about what one should value by considering his present.

I count all things to be loss (worthless) in view of the surpassing value of knowing Christ Jesus my Lord, for whom I have suffered the loss of all things, and count them but rubbish [as trash or dung] so that I may gain Christ....

What an amazing idea. So often, we humans strive for some sort of recognition or honor that we can count to our own good. This type of living is an error, and to be candid, it's something I have wrestled with all my life (probably why God consistently brings this verse to me). We want to see that the work we do, the time we spend, has merit. More so, we want to believe we are great or cool or worthy. I know I just covered this in the last chapter, but it is such a vital point that we must stress it again.

How we think on this issue becomes visible in what we do and our many choices in life. Do we blow our own trumpet to get likes and followers? Should we brag about our actions or our talents? Such can be a sad attempt find our own worth. It's as if we don't truly value our own life, while also wondering if we can make God happy enough.

God wants us to know that there is nothing you could do that actually would bring you enough merit in His eyes. Most of the time, we will fail gloriously in what we do; we humans consistently mess things up. Even the times we do well with someone, say you help another person, the tendency is to then brag about it to another or to look for that person to give you some credit for what you did. Jesus told us when we do that, in that moment, we have gained all the glory we'll get...and not really the glory we want. He warns us to even try to hide our actions from ourselves; "don't let your left hand know what your right hand is doing (Matt 6:1-4). Don't spend energy trying to get fame or have other people see you for something you are doing. We don't need to tell others; we can simply do the good things that we should do and know that God sees.

Even better, God's plan is that even though we are not worthy, He declares us as precious and worthy of His love. He comes to save us and redeem us even though we have done nothing to deserve such action. Paul is pointing out to the church at Philippi that all the supposedly great or cool things he has done are worthless.

Think about that; in case you've forgotten, Paul was a pretty amazing and successful person. He writes a ton of what we call the New Testament. He starts churches all over the eastern Mediterranean. He helps construct the initial theological understanding of what Jesus meant by His words. If anyone could make a bit claim about present value, it would be Paul. And yet, Paul is writing this letter from prison. In a few years, he is going to be executed. If you and I were advising God, we'd urge him to release Paul who clearly has talent, that God should use him as much as possible. God of course has another plan, one that we can't fully grasp, so even though Paul may have done some wonderful things, God currently is using Paul by NOT doing more mission trips, by NOT starting some more new churches.

Paul says that his present success is worthless...in view, IN VIEW of the surpassing value of knowing Christ. Wow!! Whatever else I have done that may be good or successful, it is all worthless compared to knowing Jesus. There simply isn't anything else of merit. And, again, I think the flip side is equally true. If I think I have failed or had hard times, rather than assessing those with some negative perspective, I instead should count that too as rubbish, as dung, in view of the surpassing value of knowing Christ.

Now let's look at the deeper bit to come at the end of verse 8...that Paul is desiring to gain Christ. This part is a mystery...Paul can't be saying that he, Paul, has to earn Jesus' love. He isn't saying that it's a "do this or else" kind of point. He also isn't saying "I'm not a Christian yet, so I hope to gain Christ and become such." No...he is rather reminding us of the overwhelming gift being offered to us. There is simply nothing else to compare to God's gift given freely to you.

This is the point Jesus makes when he tells the disciples that God's gift, the Kingdom of Heaven, is like someone discovering wealth in a field that he did not own. That person would go and sell everything they owned in order to purchase the field, knowing that they would have riches beyond measure (Matthew 13:44-46). So, Paul says, and urges you and I to, discard everything to gain Christ. I hope this makes you reflect back to Luke 9:23 yet again.

At this point, Paul digs deeper into the issue of walking with Jesus. He talks about righteousness and about experiencing God's power in life. This is the transition point that leads to the verses I posted for this chapter. And here, Paul takes a surprising turn; or maybe not, maybe I just don't have the depth that he has—but, you can almost see Paul pausing, wanting to make sure that he doesn't start boasting in some wrongheaded way.

I don't mean to say that I have already achieved these things.

Have you ever been around someone you know to be very successful and yet are also very humble, very grounded as a regular person? It's always so refreshing to be around someone like who just in their natural mannerisms makes you feel at ease. They have a quiet confidence that presents the same spirit as what Paul is saying here... "you may think I'm a super Christian, super successful and all that, but I tell you I know I have not fully achieved these things." Paul is modeling for us to never think you have arrived, that you are perfect. You are not. You actually WILL not be such.

But then, Paul doesn't just sit in this humility. Instead, continuing with the surprise, he drops this truth about the future.

I press on to possess that perfection for which Christ Jesus first possessed me.

I long ago memorize this in my Bible drill days from the King James: "I press toward the mark for the prize of the high calling of God in Christ Jesus." It a racing metaphor, and of course you remember I was a swimmer in my young days (and a coach early in our marriage), so the idea of staying at maximum effort, pressing forward, never letting up as you go hard toward the end of the race is something I love. I hope you girls will always be someone who strives consistently as a believer, never satisfied but rather hungry for a deeper walk, for more insight about God.

It is at this point that Paul completes the metaphor about time and how to live your life in consideration of time. "Forgetting the past [forgetting what lies behind] and looking forward to what lies ahead, I press on...."

I press on!

The events of your life can really become a heavy weight. Both our successes and our failures can really hinder our forward progress through life. Trust me, you will remember the moments that you really blew it. You'll feel badly about the time lost or missed. You will look back at the high points, and to some degree, want to live there again. Even events in the present moment, both good and bad, can become like thick vines that wrap around your feet keeping you from moving on towards the future.

God is urging you to forget those moments! Forget when you've failed. When you've dropped the ball. Don't let those memories slow your progress. Forget your successes. Don't let those high moments go to your head. They are not the culmination of what you really want to achieve.

I press on!! Yes...that is the way of the Christian. I press on toward the goal; what is the goal...it is Christ. As I have written elsewhere, the entire point of the Christian life is to become like Jesus. In all you do, in all your interactions, in all the moments with other humans, the goal is singular—become like Jesus. Of course, Paul is hinting about heaven. He is suggesting that each day is one more day on the lifelong journey. No failure nor success of yesterday causes me to stop and quit moving. The days add up. I'm now 56. That's a lot of days from when God first laid his hand on me...but I have not arrived. I have not achieved perfection. So, I must forget the past, forgetting the things that lie behind and instead look forward.

God is calling you heavenward. He is calling you home. It is a promise. There He will give each discipline the heavenly prize. You will hear "well done good and faithful servant."

Don't let your past or your present or even your future trap you. Forget the past. Don't dwell on the present. Press on! Press on! Go forward. God is calling you.

Chapter 15

I Chronicles 29:11-12—Yours O Lord, is the greatness, the power, the glory, the victory, and the majesty. Everything in the heavens and on earth is yours, O Lord, and this is your kingdom. We adore you as the one who is over all things. Wealth and honor come from you alone, for you rule over everything. Power and might are in your hand, and it is at your discretion individuals are made great and given strength.

One of the greatest challenges of the journey as a disciple is dealing with money. This becomes a challenge for young adults when they first are out on their own paying their own bills. Money is one of the potential disasters for marriages. In old age, the challenges of living on a reduced income can lead seniors into ruinous scenarios. Money is such a big deal that the Bible talks about it or uses it as an example over 2300 different times; by contrast, prayer is mentioned about 500 times. So, understanding how to handle finances as God directs is vital to your future success.

Throughout human history, the issues of wealth, of economic equity, and of the challenges of living with either riches or poverty, have confronted humans. Bottom line is that we don't do this well. There are many reasons, and a complete coverage of those issues would become a book...and you can find many books on the topic, Christian or non. I would offer, however, that this verse stands at the center of finding wisdom for anyone seeking to handle their resources.

Today, the leading guru about money management is Dave Ramsey and his Total Money Makeover. When your mother and I got married, that expert was Larry Burkett. In the months before our wedding, we read his book The Complete Financial Guide for Young Couples. I stumbled upon that book in early 1989, read it, sent it to your mother, then my fiancée, and together we determined that this teaching would be vital for us. We both have said that the lessons we learned from that book especially about budgeting was crucial to helping us navigate the first 5-7 years of marriage. In between those two leaders emerged the Christian financial guidance study by Crown ministries. It was while engaging in that study in 1996 that I was first introduced to this verse and have loved it since.

One of our current national problems is that most people either live at a level that exceeds their income, or are so unaware of their money, it disappears each month leaving them scrambling to pay bills. Those realities point toward aspects of budgeting; realize that a budget is not confining but liberating. However, rules or ideas for budgeting is not where we start. What we need is a foundation for our lives in understanding wealth. A budget or basic principles of money management do not work if I don't first understand the concepts from this verse.

Everything in the heavens and on earth
is yours, O Lord

God owns everything. That is the first principle. God is at the center of life, obviously, but even in things that may feel mundane or functional like managing our money, God is core. This verse comes from King David at the end of his life. He is working to ensure that all of the building materials are ready for his son, soon-to-be King Solomon, in order that the temple can be built in Jerusalem. The verses right before this describe all of the wealth, including thousands of gold coins and tons of silver and bronze, that has been gathered by David from the various citizens of Israel. Note that he says the people gave freely. However, David realized that there was the potential for the people to believe that they themselves had produced all of this wealth. Such a stance could lead to all sorts of issues in the future nation, especially connected to worship or ownership.

So, David states this crucial first principle in front of the people. Everything belongs to God. This isn't the only place in the Bible where this concept is mentioned. The Psalmist says, "the earth's is the Lord's." God, speaking through the prophet Haggai, says "all the gold is mine." We are told God owns "the cattle on a thousand hills." None of these ideas are simply metaphorical, but statements of reality.

This matters deeply in helping us understand how to manage our money and the things in our lives because if God owns everything, then I own nothing. Perhaps more critical is the fact that therefore, I am only a receiver and God is the One who gives. I am the one who gets something for nothing. We've seen this already with the idea of salvation, that it is not earned through anything we do, but is a gift from God. The fact of "God as giver" extends to everything in life.

So, do I have a role at all? Yes. God, in His amazing mysterious plan, chooses to involve us. We'll see more about this later connected to other areas of life, and especially related to Christian ministry, but He involves us also in this arena of money. Since I am not in control, and I own nothing, but yet realize that as I look around there are things and money clearly here in my home…well, what's up with that? The answer is that God chooses you as His partner in life managing His creation. In other words, He makes you a Trustee overseeing various parts of His world.

The old term you may have heard as it relates to Christian teaching on money is Steward. That is fine, of course, but in our modern world I think that word doesn't connect. With the way modern business and organizations are structured, the term "trustee" emerges often. A Trustee is someone assigned, usually legally such as in a will, to oversee or manage a business or an estate (money, land, the holdings of a family).

The Trustee realizes that she is not the owner of any of this material or money. Instead, it is her job to take care of the estate, or the thing "trusted," in order for it to prosper. Think of a Trustee overseeing the estate of a child whose parents have tragically passed. The Trustee is now put in control of all the wealth and land that technically belongs to the child. The Trustee needs to make sure that when the child comes of age, maybe years later, their financial standing is in good shape. The critical question of a trustee is not related to what they can do with the money for themselves, but rather "how do I ensure that the trust grows and prospers?" Keeping with that image of someone now managing the estate of a young child, that child might come to live with them. This Trustee might need a bigger house to provide a room for the child or a newer or more appropriate vehicle. Spending the money of the trust to benefit the child, even though it obviously provides a benefit to the trustee, is the right thing. However, through it all, the Trustee is aware that none of this money belongs to them.

None of your money, none of your possessions belong to you. Instead, everything belongs to God. You are merely managing the "trust." He expects you to give an account of all those things given to you, and He wants you to use them well. This is no call to false poverty. If you allowed your house to fall into disrepair or didn't buy good or enough food for yourself or family, and yet gave money away to ministry, God would not evaluate that act of giving as you have done well. Instead, He would note that you had failed to manage the trust well.

To help yourself grasp this functionally, I urge you to do a couple of steps. First, learn to use the appropriate pronouns of ownership. It's not "my guitar" but rather "God's guitar." It's not "my car," rather it's "God's car." In the Crown Ministry study, we had a task of literally writing everything in our possession as a list, which for some people in the study took pages. Then, across it, write in large words "God owns all." So, secondly, you should do that; it would surprise you perhaps just how much stuff is under your control: clothes, vehicles, electronic devices, jewelry, makeup, food, music, movies, etc...

Taking this position is vital to help you learn contentment. If I correctly recognize that I own nothing, but yet see all of these amazing things in my home, from clothes to DVDs to computers, cookware or cars...I realize how much I have been blessed. Contentment is one of our aims in life as a Christian. We can become dis-contented when we allow the circumstances surrounding our possessions to dictate your attitude. Defeat this fact by constantly acknowledging the Lord's ownership every time you purchase an item. Let me give you a simple example that you might remember from when you were young.

In the early 2000s, we had the opportunity to purchase a new car. Remember our new Chrysler van? Your mother did a ton of research to find a good vehicle and led us in making the purchase. This would be the first new vehicle that we had bought in over a decade, so it was special, and we were excited about it. On the day we picked it up, we stopped to buy dinner with you three girls in the back. All happy and fun. We got the food and helped you get set, and then we took off to drive. As soon as your mother accelerated and turned into traffic, all of your drinks spilled. Oh no! Our new car...no!! Do you remember? The tears flowed as you all dealt with embarrassment and some wet clothes. Your mother and I quickly reminded each other, "it's not our car; it's God's." Rather than going into a funk or becoming discontent about what happened, or worse yelling at you girls because the drink spilled, we laughed and understood that we all had a lot to learn about our new car.

And, just in case you think spilled drinks is no big deal, we had the same sort of thing happen to us with our first new car, except that time, less than a month after purchase, we hit a deer. Our new car was new no more. That time, I pouted. I was discontent. My thought was more of "how could you God." How could God let my new car get wrecked. But, it wasn't my car. It was His car. He owns everything. Had I thought better, I would have realized the change in attitude that I needed. Our role is to adore or worship God as the One in control, not be mad about nor attempt to contend with Him about control.

There's one more key thing I want you to see with this verse. Its perhaps not quite connected to money management, but vital, nonetheless. It is the concept that God controls what happens in our world, both now and in the future.

> *Power and might are in your hand, and it is*
> *at your discretion individuals are made*
> *great and given strength.*

David is stressing the point that not only does wealth comes from God, but also human advancement and accomplishment. David realizes this perhaps more deeply than most. He had previously just been a shepherd boy. Because he obeyed his dad and took supplies to his brothers at a battlefield, David was in place to confront the giant Goliath. Now, if we press this too far, then we'll stray into a conversation about predestination and issues surrounding how exactly God does control things. We'll leave that alone for now; just recognize that as we move ahead in our lives, it is vital to see that power and might are not ours to seek, but rather, much like with our money, we should manage the life we have been given. If God wants to lift someone up into a place of honor or authority, that's His decision to make.

Please note that simply because a Christian has not been made great or has not accomplished, isn't promoted at work or lacks fame, does not mean God is mad at them. Such isn't some indication that they have failed or sinned. There is no "name and claim it" theology in the Bible regarding money or power, thus a person being poorer than others or weaker than others in no way speaks about their faith.

All of this reflects back on what I said earlier about how most of us in this country have lost perspective and fail to see that we are rich. Many Americans remain in a state of discontent, as if we have little. We watch advertising about $75000 vehicles and $1500 phones and $2500 suits and $15000 vacations, and as we realize we don't have the money to afford those things, and we thus become embittered. Spending and living at "that level" is modeled to us as "normal," but it is not. Instead, as a people, we've lost touch with what is normal. We think AC and electricity and refrigerators and new furniture, and 4500 square foot houses are essential items, when all of those are extras, are discretionary. We are blessed to live in a time with those items which make life easier, but they aren't in some way required lest we die. Please go travel to other parts of the world; you will see that the things we believe to be "normal" are not so elsewhere. This doesn't mean we should forego an item like a refrigerator or a cell phone, but we should learn to operate in the awareness that having such is a blessing. And, for many items like certain cars or vacations or larger houses, those are simply unnecessary.

When I keep this verse firmly in mind, I remind myself that even if I live in a small house or don't have new clothes or if my phone is old, I still have all that I need. Remember how I said your mother and I believe Larry Burkett's book critically aided our marriage? In those first years I was in seminary and your mother worked a temp job making about $20,000. To manage our money took great effort and left us often in what felt like tight circumstances. We would go to the grocery store with $20 to buy enough food to last 2-3 weeks. I worked two other part-time jobs, and she put forth amazing effort to find a higher paying job. And we prayed. We prayed reminding God that we are His and that He owned everything. We believed that since He does own everything, then it's His responsibility for providing. He did. He gave us the jobs, and later, gave your mother a more fulfilling job. Through it, we learned that we could live on what He had given. We could be content even with less than others.

We did it by living simply. Simple living really deserves another chapter, as it's a vital part of managing your money. Let me just say that as I realize that God owns everything, and He provides what I need, then I need to manage the trust well so that regardless of how much I have, I don't spend frivolously.

In simple living you learn to de-accumulate. You learn to buy for usefulness, not status. You understand that you should never buy now and pay later...which often becomes pay much later, and thus pay much more due to the costs of interest. Credit becomes a false signal to avoid as it lies to you implying you can spend far more money than you actually have.

I hope you already know this lesson from your childhood. You hopefully remember how at birthdays and Christmas we would pull aside clothes and toys and items, not broken or ruined, but still useful, to give to others. Sometimes you would ask us why you had to take this step, and always it was to help teach you the premise of this verse. Today, your mother and I continue to put these principles into action.

In the end, it is okay to have possessions. And, it's okay to buy some things that you want. It's great to give gifts, even lavish at times. God Himself is a lavish giver. However, always remember "I am God's Trustee and everything I have (both possessions and money) belongs to Him."

God owns everything; we can live simply and through doing so, be a blessing to others.

Chapter 16

Matthew 11:28-30—Then Jesus said, "Come to me, all of you who are weary and carry heavy burdens, and I will give you rest. Take my yoke upon you. Let me teach you, because I am gentle and humble in heart, and you will find rest for your souls. For my yoke is easy to bear, and the burden I give you is light."

Early in my ministry years, and actually before I met your Mother, this verse captured my attention. It's one I had marked and underlined in my teen Bible. It's a mixture of metaphors that can be confusing, but as with most of these other verses that I have shown you, Jesus is sharing the best way to live as a believer.

First, obviously, is the call. Matthew places this set of verses in a chapter where Jesus is confronted with doubts from others and resistance to his call. First, we see that John the Baptist, now in prison, is no longer certain about his own declaration that Jesus was indeed the Son of God. He sends two of his disciples to ask Jesus some more questions. After that conversation (vv1-6), Jesus begins to talk to the crowd about who John was. Jesus honors John, but towards the end of this speech (from verse 7-19, but now looking exclusively at vv 16-19), Jesus starts to openly admonish the people because they mocked John.

From there, in verse 20, Jesus "began to denounce the towns where he had done so many of his miracles because they [the people of the town] hadn't repented of their sins and turned to God." As an aside, if you ever get frustrated because you aren't seeing salvations or that people you are praying for, ministering to, don't change their ways...well, remember that it happened to Jesus also. So, through the section, going to verse 24, Jesus is really bringing the denunciation. I would say he is really frustrated.

Yet, in verse 25, Jesus stops to pray. It's not, though, a prayer of hope; it's not Jesus praying that those towns or people will come to their senses through God's grace. Instead, Jesus prays a thanksgiving that God is "hiding these things [truth, wisdom, the path of salvation] from those who think themselves wise and clever." Now, later in the book, we will come back to this same hard idea when Paul talks about it in I Corinthians; we've already gotten a sense of this in the last few verses I've shown you involving Paul's life. For now, just realize that God's own plan is beyond our comprehension, and here Jesus is not pulling any punches in stating that this wisdom of God has been hidden. However, it also has been revealed "to the childlike."

So, to those childlike people, those who realize that they are not "wise and clever," Jesus then states the verse for this chapter.

Come to me, all of you who are weary and heavy-laden.

Now, he doesn't say it specifically here, but there is a tone of "who are NOT the rich and powerful." Of course, more than just rich and powerful people rejected Jesus. Every person who was poor or marginalized or weak did not become a believer, but it is true that for the person who thinks themselves wise or cool or rich...well, it's just easier to avoid God. This idea, actually, ties back to what we saw in a previous chapter where Paul warned us to not consider our actions as all that special.

So Jesus calls us to rest. Come to Him, and He will give us rest. The interesting thing is that Jesus isn't talking about physical rest, as if you are tired. Instead, it's almost the idea of "rest from the churn." Look back at the start of the chapter...we can perhaps summarize the discussion by seeing it as Jesus confronting a people in the churn to achieve or find "the better." Whether it's John and his disciples still unsure, wondering if they should seek another messiah, or its the cities where Jesus ministered, places that refused to accept his call. Instead, as the image suggests, they continued to wander and pursue whatever they hope could satiate their desires.

In the end, those people will not find rest. Not in this life, not in the afterlife. Girls, don't ever forget that the life we live now in the flesh is only the start of reality. There is more. There is an eternity in which we live, in some capacity...our souls and spirit continue. I don't mean you'll wander the earth, as if still stuck here; there are no ghosts in the way it is often told by popular tales. However, there is a spirit world and each person will either spend it in the "rest" of God's garden or in the unrest of "not God."

Jesus' offer here is that if you come to Him, you will find rest. Rest from the churn and a promised rest beyond. That's a good thing. Far too many things try to distract, try to lead us astray into wasted time, wasted years, and a wasted life. Fix your eyes directly on God and He will lead you well.

At this point, Jesus uses surprising image that, I feel, makes this verse a bit more complex. He says in v 29 to "take my yoke upon you." A yoke, as I hope you know, is a tool from the pre-mechanical agrarian world. It was a heavy wooden beam used to link two animals together for them to work, typically to pull a plow or a wagon. In other words, it is a tool of work and effort. See the mixed metaphor?

Jesus says, "I will give you rest" and then "take on this tool of work, of effort yet to come." Huh? Well, He's is not confused, that's for sure. Part of the image is what I already told you, that the "rest" he offers is not of "no work." He isn't saying if you become a Christian, you can count on a life of ease. In fact, as we have already seen in this book, he's calling us to a life of self-denial and consistently working for His name. As we shall see later, He expects us to take up a lifetime of work in His name sake, participating in the active ministry of reconciliation, being a witness and a disciple in every phase of your life. Jesus is not confused.

There's another part though which deepens the picture, and it comes from the rest of v 29. Often, on a farm, the farmer would pair a younger animal with an older animal in the yoke. The farmer was wanting the younger animal to learn the best way to do the work so that the effort would actually be easier. It would still be work, but in one sense, there would be a rest from straining or over-exertion because the younger animal would learn the right way to engage. Jesus says, "let me teach you." So, we can even imagine that we are yoking ourselves TO JESUS. That He is with us in this yoking. He is right beside us, pulling alongside. Of course, we know that Jesus will, after He goes back to heaven, leave the Holy Spirit who will reside inside each Christian. Thus, the yoke or the partner with which we will work is still God, but in the Spirit.

And what is He teaching us, the more mature wiser of the pair? To be "gentle and humble in heart." The Greek here seems to present this as "gentle," and then "humble in heart." A different reading could be "in my heart, I am gentle and humble." Regardless, as we saw when we discussed the Fruit of the Spirit verse, these are attributes that God wants us to exhibit. I don't think Jesus is saying that these two things are the only things He plans on teaching us as we stand beside Him in the yoke.

The gentle and humbleness are also part of his character that He is offering as proof that becoming yoked to Him will be okay. Take His Yoke. Let Him teach you. We are "the little children" He prayed over, so rather than being left unprotected or lacking instruction, we are invited into the yoke to be trained and protected. Wear God's yoke and "you will find rest for your souls." Why? Well, look at the last part of the verse and really commit this idea to your mind.

My yoke is easy and the burden is light.

Again, think about the Luke 9:23 verse; the call to self-denial. Each day we take up our cross, deny ourselves and die to ourselves. I don't want to hide anything from you girls. That is a difficult road to walk. Jesus told us that too; the way of Jesus is narrow, difficult, hard to walk on. It is far easier to just go with the crowd on the typical "there is no God" path of life. That way is broad, but though easy, it leads to destruction.

And yet, Jesus is saying that He will be with us, alongside, yoked, and He will show us how to walk this path. Thus, this is in fact "easy to bear." It is a light burden. Maybe I'm asking you to play a mental game here, but I don't mean to. The path of Jesus, as He said, is hard...and yet, as He is with us, it is actually easy and light. When you are going, and as you find the way hard, remind yourself of this verse. Jesus is yoked with us as we go. We have His promise to never leave us or forsake us. As we walk with Him, even through trying times, we will have rest for our souls.

The world can be a very hard and cruel place. Knowing that God is with us, Jesus yoked beside us and the Spirit residing inside of us is a good thing. It's a very good thing.

Chapter 17

I Peter 4:1a—So then, since Christ suffered physical pain, you must arm yourselves with the same attitude he had, and be ready to suffer, too.

Philippians 2:3-5—Don't be selfish; don't try to impress others. Be humble, thinking of others as better than yourselves. Don't look out only for your own interests, but take an interest in others, too. You must have the same attitude that Christ Jesus had.

Romans 12:3b—Don't think you are better than you really are. Be honest in your evaluation of yourselves, measuring yourselves by the faith God has given us

You should recognize the fact that with verse 3 of Romans 12, we've now covered the first three verses of that magnificent chapter. If you committed just those three verses to memory, you would be on solid ground for the rest of your lives as you make your way on the journey of life. And, having just told you two chapters ago that we'd spend more time in Philippians, you shouldn't be surprised to see a verse from that letter either. The theme of the last two chapters have been in this arena about attitude during life, so I thought this would be a great place to bring this vital trifecta of verses to your attention.

There are really two united themes in these three verses, so we'll take time to investigate both sides. I love these verses and quote them often. I probably have them so connected to memory because both issues are a problem for me, so God has worked overtime to try and mold me in a different perspective than my natural. So, let's dig in.

The first point is maybe the most obvious, especially in the Peter and Paul writings: we should have only one goal or one model in how to live our lives. The writer of Hebrews uses this wonderful verbiage when he writes, in chapter 12 verse 2, to "fix your eyes on Jesus." Isn't that great? Fix your eyes. Focus your gaze! The word being used there suggests the act of looking away from one thing and onto another. That's what walking as a Christian is; previously I was looking at other things to guide my life (remember the Psalm 1 passage we already reviewed), but now I am concentrating my sight on another thing to guide my life.

All three passages center on this theme of guidance and modeling. Peter and Paul both describe the idea as a mental assent in order for my life to match Jesus. Have the same mind, in other words, or let your mind be similarly thinking just like Jesus thought. I appreciate the choice of the word "attitude" as a representation of this. Let your attitude be precisely like Jesus.

Now, the two writers will look at this attitude from a different lens. Peter looks at the fact that the walk of a Christian will involve sacrifice and suffering, but his point is that it's okay. You should mentally, and physically, prepare for this, and you do that by having the same attitude as Jesus who also suffered physical plain. Peter spends a significant amount of time on the issue of suffering in his two letters, with a major focus being that we understand it will naturally come. Therefore, we should not be surprised or caught off guard when it does come. And when it does come, our attitude needs to be like what we saw in Jesus when he suffered.

Meanwhile, Paul's use of the term to his church in Philippi looks back at the earlier verses and in the song that follows in that same section. He is writing about the vital role of community, of the "one another", and that you must work consistently to foster the investment. Notice that he makes the focus mostly on yourself. He doesn't really lay the blame or the weakness of accomplishing community on the other person. So, as you live your life, this staccato list of things will guide you well:

- Don't be selfish
- Don't try to impress others
- Be humble
- Think of others as better than yourself
- Don't look out only for your own interests
- Be concerned about the interest or issues of other people

Then, Paul summarizes the concept with that one sentence.

You must have the same attitude that Christ Jesus had.

It's almost like you can see Paul saying, "do this and don't do that and please do this and look, well these things are all about how to build good relationships, and...so, do this one thing: have the same attitude as Jesus." Right after that, he breaks into a song that was perhaps a worship song for the early church that extols how, exactly, Jesus did live.

So, if I am to have the same attitude as Jesus...well, give me an example. So, Paul does provide an example by singing about that Jesus knew He was equal to God (of the same essence, the Triune Godhead), but Jesus did not consider that equality something to be grasped. Instead, He gave up His rights and humbled Himself even to death on the cross. There's that same imagery for the disciple about the cross and denial, again. Pretty obvious Paul (and this song) is reflecting what Jesus said to those who wanted to be a follower.

Our natural focus is to do the opposite of these things. We don't have the same attitude as Christ, obviously; we do think about self, first. We don't want to suffer or act in a way that denies self. We think more highly of ourselves than we want, and we typically don't think much of "the other" person. This is the human way in the basic natural world. Paul is calling us, rather, to that upside-down world that God means for His children.

Well, when Paul is speaking about the humility part, doing nothing selfish or in a conceited way, this reminds us of his verse to the church at Rome. You might take a moment here to flip back to the chapter where I explained Romans 12:2 for you. That's where Paul has said to not copy the world, to not be conformed to the world, but rather to allow God to transform your mind. He probably could have just dropped in "have the same attitude as Jesus" to nail down the point. He didn't, but it's clear Paul is on the same point as in Philippians.

Here, Paul points out that this is a warning. Again, here as in Philippians, Paul is focusing on the issue of building up the community of believers. Nothing destroys a group dynamic faster than one member of the group thinking highly of themselves. The moment someone takes this stance, then it becomes very difficult for the group to work well together. It is not easy to hide when you have a haughty attitude, carrying around the belief that you are superior to others. That person becomes a poison in the group. They usually won't pull their weight in the work or will become overly critical of others. Paul writes a similar warning about this in Galatians 6:2-3. "If you think you are too important to help someone, you are only fooling yourself. You are not that important." His blunt statement hits home.

Now, let's be clear here...we aren't saying that you need to have false humility. This isn't a statement demanding that you deny obvious gifts and talents that you have. Paul isn't focused on, or even suggesting anything about your innate abilities. There are things each of you do in which you are very talented. In a few areas, you are exceptional. That is true for each human. In some aspect of life, some talent or ability or skill, you have exceptional talent. Don't deny that. Don't downplay that in front of others. False humility is almost as annoying as arrogance.

This is why I like the list Paul gives in Philippians, and so I think that you should read Romans 12:3 in connection to Phil 2:3-5, which gives the verses better context. Add in the idea from Romans 12:2 and its even stronger. We have a natural way, the way of our flesh in which we do allow ourselves to be molded by the world. And that "way of the world" is to self-aggrandize. It is to trumpet around how great I am. The world does make it "dog eat dog" and "every person for themselves." You achieve your dreams by stepping on and over others. Don't look back or get distracted by their petty problems. Just focus on you and your own needs. That is all that matters.

No!

Have the same attitude as Jesus who didn't think his natural equality with God something to be leveraged, but instead humbled himself. He constantly thought of others first. He never wasted energy trying to impress other people.

God loves you and has already told you how valuable you are to Him when he sacrificed His own Son for you. You are of immense worth because God said so. In that truth, you can have a confidence that allows you to have the same attitude as Jesus and not be arrogant, not think more highly of yourself.

Let God transform your mind and walk in the world putting other people first. It's the best way to live.

Chapter 18

John 13:34-35—So now I am giving you a new commandment: Love each other. Just as I have loved you, you should love each other. Your love for one another will prove to the world that you are my disciples."

These next verses are ones that became more important to me as we drew close to the start of the new Millennium, about the time you all were alive. This is because your Mother and I had felt led by God to start a new Christian ministry that we ultimately decided to call Numinous. Initially, the entire point of the ministry was as a vehicle for my travelling and speaking wherever God would allow. When we started, we also began local ministry activities including speaking at schools and in 1999, we started hosting a Bible study at our home. As you know, that home study (we called it Bliss) took off and by early 2000, several in that group considered it their spiritual home, a church. Eventually, we decided to start a church using the same name as our ministry.

I had not planned to start a church. I knew at this point that I had to get to work building a methodology and strategy for this work, and I wanted it to be only centered on the Bible. That probably sounds unnecessary to say, but over the past 30 years or so, there has emerged a cottage industry of "church starts" that provide a ton of strategy and methods. To me, both then and now, I felt like a major problem for the modern US church was that it no longer was closely tied to the Bible. Instead, it has followed secular trends while using the Bible simply for the teaching material presented.

So, I spent some time writing and praying and processing about what starting a church would mean. At the center of what I believe the Bible teaches regarding the church, and what a Christian should be doing regarding their corporate experience as a Christian with others, is explained in this one verse. Now, I've written an entire other book on this, *A Numinous Hope*, where I go into a lot more depth about why I think this verse is central to a church's philosophy. I hope you read that book someday; I really wrote that book for you too. So, I won't rehash all of that connected to the theology of the church.

However, this verse is amazing and deserves mention to you as among my favorite "most important" Bible verses you should know. We've look at, in this book, what it means to be an individual Christian. That is important, but it is not the entire story. One thing, among several, that is clear about Jesus' plans is that He did not design this faith journey to be done solo. For Jesus, there really is no Christian faith without the "one another." We could talk a lot about the words used to describe the collective, but I'll leave that in *A Numinous Hope;* for now, just realize that Jesus' theology on this point can be understood simply this way. A single person who believes in Jesus and gives her life to Him can be called a "Christian." Two such people can be called "Church." In the Greek, that word is a plural expression of those who have been called out, not a building or a term for an organized structure. Thus, if I alone have been called out of darkness into light, I am a Christian. You and me together....we are Church.

This is, to me, best seen in this passage. As I hope you know, John's gospel expands massively on the history of the Passion as it relates to the last meal Jesus had with his team. The other three Gospel writers mention it and tell parts, but it's a truncated narrative. John gives us an in-depth account, starting in chapter 13. Enjoying a meal with his team, Jesus opens the conversation about his expectations for those who will follow him after that night's events.

Realize that, from one perspective, this is Jesus "last word and testament," sort of like how someone who may soon face death (perhaps in prison, or during war confronting a firing squad) is often asked if they have any "last words." Jesus is going to die, and he knows it. While clearly everything Jesus says is important, there is a sense in which we could suggest these words in chapters 13-17 are the most vital words he has to say. Certainly, that would be true if we wish to understand what Jesus meant or planned for the church, for this collective group that would follow after him. We don't get a lot of information, via the rest of the Gospels, regarding Jesus' strategy or structure or rules for the collective group, for the Church, so these chapters are like gold.

Notice the hook here—this is tremendous. It is not just "love one another." While that would be fine of course, Jesus instead says this is a brand-new command. It has never been uttered before. Thus, He adds something to the old command to love as you want to be loved. That verse or idea is what is often called, the "Golden Rule." That idea of loving each other, treat everyone, like you want to be loved or treated was at the core of my political campaign in 2019. It is a crucial concept for all of society and is in fact mentioned by several religious traditions. Jesus, though, is going deeper with his "new command."

Loving the world and loving those who are not in agreement with you was covered already back in the Sermon on the Mount

(Matthew 5-7). That is where the Golden Rule is found in Matthew's gospel. There, Jesus said to love your enemies, to love those who attack you, to love as you want to be loved. In John 13, though, he is clearly speaking only to his followers, to the embryonic church. For them, as His disciples, the expectation is jacked up a notch. With this verse, it's not just love as you wish others to love you, but love as Jesus himself loved. The theologian Leonard Sweet called this the Platinum Rule, a higher, deeper call to love than the Golden Rule.

Do you see that? Jesus is providing two things here: a way to define who is actually a disciple and a concept regarding evangelism. First, consider that this defines who actually is a believer. "Love one another as I have loved you" and hey, as a bonus, everyone will then know you are my disciples.

Your love for one another will prove to the world that you are my disciples.

Part of our problem today is that Christians are hard to discern. What makes a person a Christian? Church membership? Just a personal declaration that you are one? Baptism? Many people have no idea exactly what Christians are supposed to believe. Sadly, many Christians also don't seem to know what Christians should believe. How can anyone tell? Jesus, here, says clearly that one can tell a Christian simply by how they love other Christians. He is not talking about loving everyone in the world this way. Nope—this is to the disciples, those who would stake their claim with Jesus. Inside the collective, where relationships are hard to maintain, in that place, Jesus says you must love one another as He loves, and by that fact, the world will know you are His disciples. Amazing.

What Jesus is talking about is a credibility issue. We face problems in proving that credibility about our witness, don't we? In my discussions with people, the one issue that comes up over and over again is credibility. One young mother told me that she was a Christian, but just could not deal with going to church because no one there had any credibility. I've had students tell me in private conversations that they might consider the claims of Christianity if there was any credibility in the people who said that they were Christians. Jesus is providing us with a solution, a plan for guaranteeing our credibility.

I think you know why loving each other will prove out credibility. You have been in enough different social groups to understand that if you put 15 strangers into a room to become a group, some normal things occur. Natural affinities step in and people click with different people. Also, natural friction occurs between other people. People just don't naturally "love" each other—not over time. They can fake it for a while but after a while, the little idiosyncrasies begin to really irritate and before long, annoyances form walls between people. You may have seen that in the workplace already. At first, everyone on a team is gung-ho, ready to go. You are excited about starting the new job. When the alarm clock buzzes, you get moving with positive anticipation. Then, over the weeks and months, something happens as you consistently work with the same team of people. Friction, disagreement, frustration and often disillusionment. That is what naturally happens. Jesus is saying that by breaking that cycle, we demonstrate that something beyond natural is at work here. What that is can only be a spiritual God-thing and that love will point to Jesus.

As we love one another as Jesus loved us, that discipleship proof emerges. These strangers share life together. When someone is in need, others rush to fill the void. They will even sell their own possessions to give that money to one another. You will be patient with the weirdness of another because you recognize that others are being patient with you. Conflict is not avoided but worked through. Reconciliation is the watchword of the group, and there is intentionality about engagement. Others, on the outside, see this and realize that this can't be through human effort alone. Even the most determined team, say a sports team or a group trying to serve in some civic way, over time, breaks apart due to the natural human divisiveness that emerges. Here, this collective group of believers is in for the long haul.

It is in that moment that Jesus' second point comes out. Though this book isn't about evangelism, I hope you note that if you will take all of these verses to heart and truly live in God's way, others will notice. Jesus is counting on that. The Christian SHOULD be living in such a way as to have others notice...probably noticing how weird you are living. But rather than some evangelistic program you need to memorize or going door-to-door trying to talk someone into believing, Jesus gives us another path. His strategy is so simple that I fear most church leaders still dismiss it. Yet, for all of my life, the American church has been losing ground and losing credibility, and I remain convinced it is because of this point. Jesus provides how Christians can have that credibility; make sure you also look at John 17, especially verses 20-21 to see his second part of the mission of the church that gives another level of credibility.

Jesus gives us a simple command (note...not simplistic; this isn't easy, as we know from the other things I've shown you): just love every other Christian no matter how annoying they are or how much they have some characteristic that bugs you. And, how are we to love? As He loved us. In case that part isn't clear, two chapters later in John 15:9-17, He makes it abundantly clear. He loved us by dying for us.

There is no greater love than to lay down one's life for one's friends.

This is agape love. The love of sacrifice. The love of putting the other first. The love of choosing what is best for the other even to the point of the choice harming you.

Can you see how this attitude is connected to the verses of the previous chapter? Or, maybe better stated, can you now see what is necessary in order to pull of the "have the same attitude as Jesus" concept? We must love as Jesus loved. We must agape the other who walks alongside us in the Christian journey. Jesus' love example yet again loops us back to Luke 9:23. He is going to die for us. And now we are commanded to love one another the exact same way.

Note, He does not say to love that way to "your best friends in the church" or to "those believers who agree with you on all theology" or "everyone BUT those people who do or say that thing you don't like." NO! His command is simple and comprehensive. If a person claims to be a Christian, then we are commanded to interface with that person under the guidance of this brand-new command about love. That action we take will prove, one way or the other, our own faith stance.

The world is watching. So is Jesus.

Chapter 19

II Corinthians 5:18-20a—And all of this is a gift from God, who brought us back to himself through Christ. And God has given us this task of reconciling people to him. For God was in Christ, reconciling the world to himself, no longer counting people's sins against them. And he gave us this wonderful message of reconciliation. So we are Christ's ambassadors....

Early on in the ministry of Numinous, people would ask me about evangelism. I suppose they wanted to hear what our methodology was going to be. Oh, they wouldn't inquire necessarily as direct as that, but in general, based on the previous chapter where I explain about the mission of the church (love one another), they wondered if I thought about evangelism at all. I do...often.

Where I differ though is that I will say that responsibility is NOT the task of "the church." Note my little air quotes around the word. Maybe I need to say more here (again, you can read *A Numinous Hope* for more depth about my theology of church), but as I briefly mentioned, today we know about the concept of the institution called church. It is an organization, with jobs and salaries and buildings. People look to, or at, the church to accomplish or do certain things. This has been developing for centuries now, but to me, along the way, that idea of a formalized institution has departed from anything that the Bible talks about. As such, many things that we read in the Bible that an individual believer should do somehow has become the concern of the church. Well, this task of evangelizing is like that; it is the task or mission of the individual Christian.

Yes, I get it. I am splitting hairs a bit, but I think that differentiation is vital. The reason why is because for many Christians, they think that as long as their church is "doing evangelism" (or they might say "doing missions"), then they, the individual, is good. Sort of a "accomplishment by proxy," if you will. However, that is not what the Bible describes. In one sense, I would suggest that most everything you can read about "The Church," as an institution that exists in the modern world is not in the Bible.

The reason I bring it up for you girls is because this is a concept you need to get locked in regardless of what others think, despite what some church may teach. I actually think most Christian leaders agree with my point, and that the bigger challenge is definitions and words. In any case, here's your focus ladies. If God has given a mission to the collective group of believers, as I explained last chapter, then He has also given a mission to each individual Christian.

This individual mission provides the other half of the picture we are painting of how I hope and pray you live. The collective mission of your journey with other Christians is the one half—as a group, our entire focus is to love each other and be unified, displaying the actions portrayed in Acts 2: teaching of the apostles, fellowship, worship, prayer, community, sharing resources. Yet, the individual believer also has a job to do. It's just that (as we've attempted to show) the church collective institution has usurped that mission and in doing so, lost its own purpose.

One member of the Numinous church (well actually part of the earliest gathering in that Bible study in my home) wrote this to me once: "OK, so all these things that I have considered to be jobs of the church (jobs that we do in the buildings) are really jobs of the body, individually. It's MY job to seek the lost, not my church's. We all just have to keep pulling each other up to the next level."

Correct!! So, here in Paul's second letter to the city of Corinth, we are told that we have a task, a mission, as individual Christians. It is a great responsibility to represent a King, a power greater than yourself. Certainly, here (as in Matthew 28:18-20) plural pronouns are used to express that this applies to all individuals in the group. And also just as certainly, there is nothing wrong with a group of Christians actively doing something for the purpose of sharing about Jesus or doing some service project together. Yet, overall, the thrust here is toward each individual.

It is as if Paul is saying here, "We, each of us, are Christ's ambassadors. Even if your Christian buddy does not do this, does not go out, you are Christ's ambassador." Even if other Christians around me fail at this, God expects me to do my part. If, to use the language of Matthew 28, if other Christians do not go into all the world nor do not make disciples, I am still expected to go. I must accomplish this singularly through the actions of my life, and alone will stand before God to give an account of what I did with the time He gave me.

You should quickly tell the difference between this and the "one another" nature of the church command and mission. I cannot accomplish "love one another" without "an other" Christian. I cannot be in unity with others when I am in isolation. This is the mission of the collective group. It can only be done with others. Here, though, in this verse, I see that regardless of the others, I have a task to undertake. Of course, there is nothing wrong with a church giving concern for how it, collectively, represents God. Still, as you can see from Paul's writing, the focus of the verse is to the individual.

Amazingly, for some reason, God has refrained himself from personally entering this fray of evangelism (since Jesus ascended) and instead has chosen to work through us, his created beings. Of course, He has not left us alone, having given each Christian His Spirit, so in essence, He does reside with us. Yet, He will never override our own free will, so He is in that way constrained. If we, knowing we have a mission and a purpose, refuse to go through with our task, then God is bereft of hands and feet to accomplish His great redemptive work.

The Apostle Paul is not the only one to share this news. Jesus himself told us this in his own wonderful style, and the teaching from the Sermon on the Mount is a vital pairing. In Matthew 5:13-16, the gospel writer begins to share with his readers the great message Jesus shared sitting on a hill in Galilee. After starting with the long list of blessings to those who follow him, He then shifts gears to get to the heart of the message—the mission or job of anyone who makes the claim to be one of God's chosen children. His first word to the crowd is a command to those who wish to follow Him, a teaching about our task.

> *You are the salt of the earth. But what good is salt if it has lost its flavor? Can you make it salty again? It will be thrown out and trampled underfoot as worthless. You are the light of the world—like a city on a hilltop that cannot be hidden. No one lights a lamp and then puts it*

under a basket. Instead, a lamp is placed on a stand, where it gives light to everyone in the house. In the same way, let your good deeds shine out for all to see, so that everyone will praise your heavenly Father.

To those Jewish listeners it should not have been a surprise. From the time of Abraham, the promise of God was that the entire world would be blessed and in communion with Him through His chosen people. So now, Jesus is in one sense reminding them of their task. Looking through Gentile, Christian eyes, we can see that the same command lies upon us. And that command? Much as what Paul wrote, that we have an individual mission to impact the world. We are to be the salt of the earth and the light of the world. Into this dark and tasteless world, we are sent with the message of hope. Individually, that is our task.

Think of your own life—it's possible that where you work, where you go to school, where you live, you are the only Christian there. Of course, you might not be the only person who calls themselves a Christian, but you might easily be the only one there with the knowledge about the task. You might be the only one not living in some fear of the world or in some sense relying only on the professional leadership of the church. Thus, you might solely be God's only voice there. His only means of shining a light.

Part of the challenge here lies in how often most people think of the tasks of religious activity belonging mostly, or even only, to the paid professional staff person. Wrong. That idea of some division between official "clergy" and "laity" (to use older terms for paid staff vs regular people) is simply not in the Bible. Yes, there are leaders of Churches and Christian ministry, and they do have leadership roles to play, but most of the calls for ministry action from Jesus are to each and every believer.

Part of the problem is that we refuse to believe what God has told us--that this world, the physical world is really not the real world. He tells us that there is a real world, a spiritual world that is eternal currently existing around us and that only those with His spirit can see it. The story of *The Matrix* again provides a great illustration. We think we are awake in a real world when all along, we are sleepwalking through a dream world. We think the job we do is somehow our real job. I'm a painter, a teacher, a lawyer, etc... and in that, we then come to conflict when we think about ministry. "How can I do ministry and do my job at the same time?"

I mentioned this movie back when I explained the Romans 12:2 passage. When the older guide Morpheus, speaks to the protagonist Neo about grasping the matrix, he told him that one could not simply be told. Instead, you have to experience it. In that same exchange, Morpheus continues to say, "What is real? How do you define real? If you are talking about what you can feel, what you can smell, taste or see, then real is merely electrical signals interpreted by your brain."

We know from Paul's writings to the Corinthian church, we actually are living in a setting where we've had "the wool pulled over our eyes." I will write more on this in an upcoming chapter, so for now, just be alert that often we do believe that this is the real world when all along God is telling us that this is merely a starting place. As a theologian I appreciate states it this way: we are not fleshly humans who die and then have a spiritual transformation; we are instead spiritual beings having a fleshly human moment.

So, all along, God is begging us to understand that as one of His disciples, we are placed on a mission. That mission is our true job and the thing we do to make money is merely our cover. Read the verse again; this is our prime directive:

And God has given us the task of reconciling people to him. For God was in Christ, reconciling the world to himself, no longer counting people's sins against them. This is the wonderful message he has given us to tell others. We are Christ's ambassadors....

It's as if we are part of a grand large undercover operation to overthrow the current ruler of the earth. He (our enemy) thinks he is immune to attack, but he does not know that we know he is merely an interloper and that the real King of the world has already invaded and is currently raising up troops. This real King sends us to all manner of places and environments to begin to spread his message of love, grace and hope. For most of us, we do this undercover—to the world and the false king, we are merely construction workers, bus drivers, doctors, secretaries, actors, social workers or professors. To the King though, we are his ambassadors of love.

It really is quite simple when you think about it and it should give you real gladness to know that your current job, no matter how little you get paid or if you feel appreciated or not, is not the culmination of your life. It's just your cover, your way into part of the world, your place to work your real job of being his representative.

God wants us to take the red pill just as Neo did in *The Matrix* to see the real world for what it is. He wants us to understand that we have an individual mission that is critical. He wants us to understand the value that each of us has in our place of service.

Remember you are not of this world and deep inside you is a longing to return home. You watch the eastern sky hoping for His return, but seeing it not, you return with hope to your task, to your cover. And all the while, you look always for the chance to perform the real task. In disguise, you work hard, as unto the Lord and you perform the best you can in an attempt to gain more credibility with those around you. As you do, you gain the confidence of those around you, "your world" and as you work act as salt and light. They will notice.

They will hear of your love for others, those like you and those who are different, and they will be amazed. They will begin to see that you must be a disciple of the King. They will see the unity of the community of faith that you belong to and long deeply in their hearts for that kind of relationship. They will silently understand that the One you follow must have come from God. They will notice that when you are around, the atmosphere seems to taste different. They will begin to see how the darkness recedes from you when you pass by. They will finally begin to ask questions or begin to share their life with you, perhaps not asking directly, but hoping inwardly that you notice their longing. They are waiting for you to fulfill your task and then begin to teach them about that same task. That's when you'll remove the mask, just like the actors in *Mission Impossible*. You'll show them why you REALY are there...to help them find the Answer for life, Jesus Christ.

Chapter 20

Psalm 119:105--Your word is a lamp to guide my feet and a light for my path.

In 2015, as Numinous was winding down as a church, I began a personal study of this Psalm, the longest chapter in the Bible. I taught it to the church, but the genesis of this for me was a study for my own benefit. You can never examine God's word too much. That study ended up a devotional Bible study book, which hopefully you've read already: *A Love Ode: A Devotional Study of Psalm 119.* It is a wonderful chapter of devotion to God's law. This is the kind of chapter that stands alone in the Bible that you can read over and over, a wonderful choice for the meditation that we've talked about previously.

This verse, however, was a favorite of mine before I did the study. You probably know it well. This is where part of the title for this book came from. It's one of the most famous of the verses in the Bible. For some people, perhaps the King James Version will sound better for you:

Thy word is a lamp unto my feet,
and a light unto my path.

That is certainly how I memorized it, and expresses the thrust of the entire Psalm: God's law, His precepts will direct you in how to live.

We've been looking at the "how do I know how to live" concept through the entire book, and this verse again becomes foundational. You need answers to some issue or question in life? Psalm 119:105. Curious about some confusion in your life, whether internally or with others? Psalm 119:105. Since we are in Psalms, remember when I introduced you to the brilliance of Psalm 1. Remember, it described the person living life well as "whose delight is in the law of the LORD, and who meditates on his law day and night." Verse 105 takes the entire idea of Psalm 1 and distills it down into just the one verse. God's law, His word is a lamp to guide you.

Psalm 119 is actually 22 distinct sections, written as an acrostic poem based on the letters of the Hebrew alphabet. This verse is the first verse of the section based on the letter "nun." It is verses 105-112, and I have found that one can gain a deeper insight by reading each of the sections as a unique or separate expression. That's how I wrote the other book, to be a daily Bible study of 27 days, with the 22 sections the core of the study. So, here, if we want to more deeply grasp verse 105, we need to look at the rest of the section around that verse.

What we can see is that the Psalmist is expressing his deep love for God's ways. This is brought up again and again through the entire work. And yes, I know that as Christians, there is a sense in which we are no longer bound to the "law" as far as trying to obey it to get to heaven. Yet, as you hopefully know through a deeper study of the New Testament, Jesus wasn't simply rejecting the law for something better or easier. Instead, as He told the religious leaders, He was looking at, devoted to the "weightier [or deeper or heavier] matters of the law." Jesus wanted His followers to realize that there is an even deeper calling, a harder path to walk, than the law. Again, not a rejection, like "the law is terrible," but rather in a "wow...the law expresses something deep and difficult and devotional about the call to be one of God's people."

So, again and again, the Psalmist expresses his great love or devotion for the law. At points he states that the law is more valuable than life itself, which of course sounds a lot like what we saw Jesus saying in Luke 9:23. Here, in vv 106-110, the Psalmist lays out some of the life experiences or moments in which we will still be expected to follow God's ways.

--Even through suffering (v. 107)
--Even when life is praiseworthy (v. 108)
--Even though life hangs in the balance (v. 109)
--Even facing opposition who will attempt to do me harm (v. 110)

The demand from God in the New Testament--"if you will be my disciple"--remains the same, remains in force in every circumstance. You and I are called to submission and obedience in each and every circumstance. How is this possible, that someone will stay obedient in these situations? Well, once again the love of God's word is brought up to provide this answer in verse 111.

Your laws are my treasure;
they are my heart's delight.

This concept of God's law being a delight, a pursuit of joy for my heart, is one of the major themes of the entire chapter. This thought was something I had not really noticed before. Perhaps I was simply too immature to understand when I was younger. Maybe it was my upbringing which did center a lot on obedience to the law, whether of the society or of my parents. "Failure to obey" brought pain and punishment, so for me, obedience was akin to AVOIDING punishment. That's fair enough, but it is not at all what the Psalmist is writing about here.

Thus, in verse 111, the writer is not saying we endure all those challenges to avoid punishment from God's rules, but that we will obey BECAUSE of the love. The law is a treasure. They are my heart's delight. I LOVE these ways of God. Through that love, then, we remain "determined." And determined for how long, to what end? He says "determined to keep your decrees to the very end."

I hope you girls feel that passion and determination. Transitioning from a "have to" mindset to a "love of my life" mindset is vital to really make your way on this narrow road. God desperately wants to journey with you, but not as a taskmaster or overlord. He wants to be your heart's desire. He wants you to look forward to the time with Him.

In that way, then, His word becomes that lamp and light. The imagery is so simple. We've all walked in the dark, whether outdoors or to the bathroom. I bet you remember times we lost power after major hurricanes, perhaps the 2004 experience. During the day, it was fine, right? Then at night, we use candles or flashlights even though we should have known the hallway and sections of our small house well. You each wanted your own flashlight or lantern so you could have light that you controlled. You didn't want to walk in any darkness. Each of you initially slept with a nightlight just in case you woke up. Your mother and I didn't want you to awake in total darkness.

God doesn't want you to walk in darkness now. This is why He has told us that He will be with us. Think back to when I showed you the Joshua 1:9 verse where God urges us to be courageous, to have no fears because He is with us. God is our light, in His person and in His revealed laws. In John's Gospel, he starts out his writing with a beautiful prologue in which he describes Jesus. There he writes that Jesus "gave life to everything that was created, and his life brought light to everyone. The light shines in the darkness and the darkness can never extinguish it."

The apostle Paul writing in Romans explains that because of our choice to become a disciple of Jesus, then "you are controlled by the Spirit...so you have not received a spirit that makes you fearful slaves; instead you received God's Spirit when He adopted you as His own children." Thus, the light of Jesus now lives within you to guide you through the Holy Spirit.

Jesus wanted this to be clear to all of us, so in His last meal with the disciples, he gives a long explanation as to how He was going to provide the Holy Spirit to each of us. In chapters 13-17 of John's Gospel, He lays out key aspects of the role of the Spirit, who Jesus calls our Advocate and our Comforter. In chapter 16, Jesus explains "When the Spirit of truth comes, he will guide you into all truth. He will not speak on his own but will tell you what he has heard. He will tell you about the future. He will bring me glory by telling you whatever he receives from me."

God does not want us stumbling around in the dark, unguided. He has provided us a lamp and a light. The word of truth provides us the way forward regardless of what we confront. We have the Holy Spirit living within us to help us understand. He guides us with directions received directly from Jesus.

Oh my dear children...the world certainly can feel confusing. There are many issues and challenges that we have to discern our best choice going forward. Sometimes the "path we seek" is about the right words to say. Other times it is about where to position ourselves relative to societal issues. Many times we need guidance for building the best relationships. And yes, often, we just need to know practical decisions like which job to take or what city to move to.

Through it all, God offers you a flashlight to guide your steps. I pray you take it up and use it.

Chapter 21

Philippians 4:11-13—Not that I was ever in need, for I have learned how to be content with whatever I have. I know how to live on almost nothing or with everything. I have learned the secret of living in every situation, whether it is with a full stomach or empty, with plenty or little. For I can do everything through Christ, who gives me strength.

I told you we'd come back to Philippians. This passage is not only one of my favorites but one of the most important to help you navigate your future life. As we have seen from the start, there is no easy road for the Christian disciple. Historically this has been true and deeply understood. However, over the past 30-50 years in the USA (and maybe in "The West" more generally, even including places like Japan), a devious myth has taken hold to suggest that life can actually be easy, comfortable, and even luxurious. As you girls navigate further in your adult lives, it is paramount to your future success to maintain a grip on the historical truth about the challenges of life.

Learning about that myth and the subsequent solution is important for your future regardless about Christianity, but for the believer its perhaps more vital. I'll come back to that; just understand that all of life takes a maximum effort. Do you remember in *The Hamilton* musical where the song speaks of Alexander Hamilton writing as if he was running out of time? They wondered, in the song, "Non Stop" about his stamina and output.

> *Write day and night like you're running out of time?*
> *Everyday day you fight, like you're running out of time.*

He was seen as an anomaly, and cast against Burr, we are shown a nice depiction between the effort life takes. This same pursuit of excellence is evident in others famous through history like Napoleon, Alexander the Great, even one of Hamilton's many political enemies, John Adams. Today, you see it in sports more obviously with great athletes pursuing aggressive workouts during their off-season in order to be as physically fit as possible, for as long as possible. "The man is non-stop."

What do these great people know? Well, perhaps first, that time is not promised to us. Even deeper though, I think they realize the simple truth that talent is never enough. Life demands raw effort put out over a prolonged amount of time. Hamilton wasn't necessarily smarter than Burr, but Burr didn't go at it at the same pace. Now, we can note that many of these people can become fanatical in the pursuit to the detriment of important relationships or even their own health.

I worry about this some myself as I think about your childhood. When you were little, I was managing two fulltime jobs (Valencia and Numinous) while also writing my books and fronting our rock band, Anodyne. I remember one student asking me how in the world I had so much output. As I told that student, I simply don't stop. But, looking back, I can see that maybe I should have dialed back some things in order to spend more time with you.

Still, the point initially in this chapter is to say that life takes work, diligent effort over time. The Bible references this elsewhere; Paul brings it up in Colossians 1:29, talking about how he goes about his work for Jesus with consistent effort and energy. In the Greek there, the verse describes Paul to be at "work to exhaustion, labor with wearisome effort, striving with athletic effort, tireless exertion, continual effort, according to the effectual working of God's power working effectively in me."

See all of those ideas? "work to exhaustion," "labor with wearisome effort," "striving," "tireless exertion," "continual effort." That is the point Paul is suggesting here, that we go non-stop for the Lord.

Over the past decade, the sickness of our country is clear. We believe luxury, comfort and ease are the norm. They are not! If you can at least get that fact locked in, you will be ahead of the crowd. This reality is important so that you don't fall prey to disenchantment or bitterness about whatever your future brings. For many, their anger at the current setting of their lives is really evidence that person has bought into the myth about ease, a commentary about this illness in our country. Expecting ease but finding as history tells us that life is a challenge, some people then look for someone to blame. If you start with a correct understanding of the norm of life, that it is hard and fraught with challenges and disappointments, that it can be short and no time nor any success is promised to you, then you won't confront the issue of false expectations.

Paul expresses this in the first part of the passage. He is telling the church at Philippi to not worry about him. They don't need to worry, he notes, because he has learned how to be content. Oh, my dear children, if you can just grasp this concept. Contentment is the opposite feeling of the disappointment over false expectations. The Greek words express the idea of being content regardless of any circumstance. This is critical; too many say, in essence, that they will be content as long as they deem the circumstance fair, or at least what they expected.

Paul then takes the idea into the realm of money. I love this part because for Americans, or at least the ones I know, money is the key data point as I noted in the Chronicles passage. If they have money, and especially discretionary income, then they can deal with other frustrations. If they believe that they don't have enough money, then no other positive in life will satiate their annoyance. This is perhaps the main reason I latched onto this verse in the early days of Numinous. Hopefully you know the story well.

Your mother and I were serving as the Student Pastor for teens and college kids at First Baptist Church Winter Park. We had started in 1995 and eager for a future there. I had already been making plans for mission trips, for student leadership long into the early 2000s. Suddenly, in 1998 things changed and the entire church staff was told to find new positions. After a lot of prayer and consideration, we decided to launch the ministry that became Numinous. To do that meant leaving a very solid middle-class salary (roughly $55,000 including insurance and retirement money), the highest salary we'd ever made in our 10 years of marriage. Yet, we stepped out in faith, started the ministry, and I attempted to raise financial support. While doing that, I also worked part-time jobs while your mother raised you girls. I was given a part-time job by some wonderful Christian men who let me work with their construction company, and between that and some financial contributions to the ministry, was making roughly $22,000.

This wasn't the first time we had confronted a miniscule income. As I told you earlier, in the early years of our marriage, your mother worked as our only income provider while I was in seminary. We had a very tight income and would go to the grocery store with a $20 bill and make it work. This time in

1998, though, we had two daughters and, in a little more than a year away, a third child on the way. We truly experienced Paul's point:

> *I know how to live on almost nothing or with everything. I have learned the secret of living in every situation, whether it is with a full stomach or empty, with plenty or little.*

The "secret of living" regardless of whether we find ourselves in humble means or in prosperity. So, as your mother and I worked day and night to bring this vision to life, we could not allow ourselves to either grow weary in the work NOR disenchanted with our financial situation. How is that possible?

Paul tells us with his closing note. "I can do everything with Christ." As a boy, I memorized it this way:

> *I can do all things through Christ who strengthens me.*

Regardless of the situation, I can make it through this day. Jesus is with me. He strengthens me. By placing my focus on Jesus, rather than the circumstances, I walk forward. I keep courage. I am confident in spite of what the context of my current life looks like. Because I know Jesus gives me strength I can be like Joshua, to be of good and strong courage. What a wonderful promise this verse is. Commit it to memory. Whatever life throws at you, you can do it! Jesus strengthens you and me.

You will have challenging times. All of life is this way. Sometimes the challenges will come in relational issues or on the job. Your children or your own health may become difficult. That is not the time to whine and moan as if you somehow have been cheated. Yes, of course, it is fine to cry and lament, especially to God. There isn't some sort of call to stoicism. Yet when you have a firm grip on the idea that all of life is meant to demand effort along the way, then you won't have misconceptions.

Moreover, as a Christian, as we have already seen, you are called to a life of denial, but with God walking always beside us. This is not just denial for denial's sake or to be some sort of martyr about your life, but to see the life with Christ as the supreme way. Remember what we read from Paul in this same letter to Philippi? I count everything as rubbish, as trash, compared to the surpassing value of knowing Jesus! So, Jesus calls us as disciples to follow Him in a life where I daily carry my cross. This is no life of "woe is me," but rather with gladness, with joy...understanding the "surpassing value" of being with Jesus. Thus, in that mindset, our actual financial situation matters none at all.

I find contentment regardless of the situation. I know how to live in a faith position when things are going well, when financially I am experiencing increase. I know how to live in a faith position when things are not strong financially, when I am experiencing lack. This is an important truth to lock in so that you can then manage your life, especially financially. If you know this is the plan, then taking time to budget is not some kill-joy task but rather your normal view of taking good care of whatever God has given you.

The choice to live simply, to pursue moderation comes naturally, and not as a "boo—have to or die" mentality. Moderation is simply what a good faithful trustee does with their finances and situation. You do it because you know what it feels like to live with little, and yet still give all to God (remember the story of the widow putting in her pennies for the offering to God). It's all His anyway, and He cares for you. So, you manage it well and still live giving to others. And when you perhaps later find yourself with much, with financial excess, you keep living this way with balance and simplicity. You don't suddenly start spending money wastefully, buying more of everything which is a gluttony even if the purchase isn't food. You know even then that you give it all to God, and that He still owns it all and He cares for you. He has given you plenty so that you can be a bigger blessing to others.

You can do this, confronting anything that comes your way, because Jesus gives you strength.

Chapter 22

Isaiah 50:7—Because the Sovereign Lord helps me, I will not be disgraced. Therefore, I have set my face like a stone, determined to do his will. And I know that I will not be put to shame.

Somewhere in the middle of our journey with Numinous, things got very hard. Lots of tears, late night conversations, disappointments and challenges. Yes...everything I just wrote to you about finding contentment in the hard times as well as the times of plenty came to fruition. I will say this was close to our first decade in, so for about 10 years, things had moved forward well. It hadn't been perfect of course, not without some issues, but overall things felt good. Then, suddenly, it just wasn't. Everything I wrote to you from the last chapter was now in my face. How would I react?

In that time, God took me to this passage and it really became a touchstone over these past years. You may recall seeing it in my email signatures when I wrote "On Mission Confident507." The concept of confidence in the end of the story became a vital point of my personal journey of faith.

Clearly the verse, and the walk for a Christian, is focused on grit. We've seen throughout that Jesus' call to us is one that isn't easy. He makes this no secret. That he is so bold with the cost of discipleship, and yet the message of evangelism is so often watered down to some simple easy thing has long confronted me. Certainly, the offer of God is clear and easy...choose through faith to believe that He is and that's it. John 3:16 stuff—"anyone who believes in Jesus will have eternal life." There's nothing you have to do to earn salvation or God's good graces. And yet, as we have seen, the journey of the person who believes will be challenging, narrow, not part of the popular crowd and demanding a life of sacrifice in order to gain not the world but preservation of your soul.

Grit is something that has come up more often in the past decade in the USA (2010-2020). I think it is because we have become addicted to ease, as I wrote about in the last chapter. If a person grows up in a society in which the message is that life should have little challenge, then that person fails to ever develop stamina or perseverance. I have seen this in the years of my teaching, especially during the time I worked in professional education at Valencia College. So often, the main lesson I taught the students was that most everything in life takes diligent effort, usually over a prolonged time period. It is not enough to just muscle up some energy for a short period, say a day to study or a weekend to write a paper; instead grit is demanded so that the person puts forth consistent work over weeks and weeks.

However, my own life shows that even if a person is doing this, they can become tired and discouraged. That is where I was finding myself as 2008-2010 was happening. Your mother and I had put forth that "consistent work" over the years. From one point of view, things had moved ahead well; through the ministry, many lives had been impacted. I felt like the message of God was faithfully being expressed. And yet, from another point of view, all the effort had not really amounted to "great success." I wrote in my journal in 2011 that "Everyone seems really tired. The elders seem really tired. The elders seem really engaged with a lot of other stuff."

Towards the end of the movie *The Return of the King,* Frodo says, "How do you pick up the threads of an old life? How do you go on... when in your heart you begin to understand... there is no going back? There are some things that time cannot mend... some hurts that go too deep... that have taken hold."

How indeed? You can't go back to relive moments or try to make different choices. You must go forward, but how? How do you learn to be you, in this new body, as a new person just understanding your changing circumstances? If everything you have ever done or said has been so through the matrix of believing certain things about your future, how then can you do or say anything now if the evidence of your experience does not match your hopes?

What you must have in that moment is a foundation. God is that foundation. As I wrote in another journal entry from that same time period, "There still is a God. You've made this proclamation before. It must be true, or you indeed are fully lost. That is an abyss you cannot slide down. There is a God. He still has the universal purpose, mission and goal that have been universal from before."

Because the Sovereign Lord helps me,
I will not be disgraced.

So, because the Sovereign Lord helps me, is with me, still loves me and has plans that involve me, I will not be disgraced. The Hebrew word there can also be translated to be "ashamed" or "humiliated." I will not be humiliated. I will not be ashamed. Yes, in the eyes of the world, your choices and words can end up where others in the world think you are disgraceful. They might think you should be ashamed or that you should feel humiliated for having such a ridiculous idea or hopes. Yet, God is with you and helps you, thus...not disgraced, ashamed or humiliated. And, as Gandalf says to Frodo in another context, "that is a comforting thought."

With that truth in hand, then what? Become determined! "I have set my face like a stone." Another translation of the Hebrew states "I made my face like flint." Of course, I am sure you see the point. Your focus is so certain that you are like a rock. One can move a rock, certainly, and with a pick and hammer, you can split a rock, but you can't simply reshape a rock like you can dirt or wood. The rock doesn't move. Or, to quote another movie we all love, the Emperor in *Mulan* dismisses the threat against him by saying, "no matter how the wind howls, the mountain cannot bow to it."

With the confidence that God, the Sovereign Lord, helps you in all circumstances, we refocus our mind in a strong determination to take another step, to live another day. This verse is another of Isaiah's prophecies about Jesus. The verse before talks about this person, the one speaking, being beaten and allowing his beard to be pulled out. This happened to Jesus, and is allowing this to happen. Jesus could have decided that He did not want to continue on the road set before Him. In His prayer in the Garden of Gethsemane, He is debating internally whether to go forward. Jesus asks God to remove "the cup" that was being offered to drink, meaning, take away the option of crucifixion and provide another method. Yet, in the end, Jesus chooses to go forward with the plan that God has set in motion.

Just like Jesus, Isaiah declares that this one in chapter 50 knows the Sovereign Lord will help him, go with him, therefore, he will set his face like flint. At this point the New Living Version adds a phrase of context to highlight this notion of continuing on the path of obedience. That phrase of "determined to do His will" is not in the Hebrew, but it is the point of the words. You can see this coming from verse four; the speaker has been given a task, words to say and things to do, and now, even though facing trials and tribulation, forward in obedience to God's will is the only way.

I love how the verse concludes. In fact, this part is what really initially grabbed me, providing me the idea of my little catchphrase *"On Mission Confident507."* I know that regardless of how things look, no matter how bad or overwhelming it may seem

I know that I will not be put to shame.

That mission that God provided (v. 5—"The Sovereign Lord has spoken to me"), with His words of wisdom as direction (v.4—"The Sovereign Lord has given me His words of wisdom"), will be accomplished as long as I stay the course. No matter what others think or how the world would assess its viability, shame will not be the situation. The Apostle Paul, writing to the church in Philippi in Greece says something similar (Phil 1:20): "For I fully expect and hope that I will never be ashamed, but that I will continue to be bold for Christ, as I have been in the past. And I trust that my life will bring honor to Christ, whether I live or die." You can see both his determination (will continue to be bold) and hope (trust that my life will bring honor). Paul and Isaiah are talking about the same concept.

Of course, you know that now, as I write this is the crazy year of 2020, Numinous as a functioning entity is closed. We heard God tell us to bring the ship into port, and all were released to go forward with the new insight they have gained. Most of the members had been with your mother and I for nearly two decades. Each person moved on in their lives, guided by God into new directions, and great ministry has happened through the work of the Numinous family. That includes you girls! And meanwhile, your mother and I have continued on the path and work God first set before us when, individually, He called us to His side.

The world could conclude that we failed with Numinous. The world could suggest that we didn't accomplish the task faithfully because we aren't actively on the mission field like we were when your mother and I first met. However, we have set our face like flint, determined to do His will each and every day. And though the enemy of our faith might suggest otherwise, I know that I nor your mother will be put to shame. God will faithfully stand with us and continue to use us as He wishes.

As you go through hard times of struggle that challenge your faith, as you go through easy times of great success that point to distraction, always remember this verse. That path indeed is narrow and difficult. The walk of the believer is one of self-denial and sacrifice. At times it will appear hopeless or pointless; it is neither! The Sovereign Lord helps you! He is with you. Refocus your determination and be the mountain in the midst of a roaring wind.

You will not be put to shame!

Chapter 23

Ephesians 6:10-18—A final word: Be strong in the Lord and in his mighty power. Put on all of God's armor so that you will be able to stand firm against all strategies of the devil. For we are not fighting against flesh-and-blood enemies, but against evil rulers and authorities of the unseen world, against mighty powers in this dark world, and against evil spirits in the heavenly places. Therefore, put on every piece of God's armor so you will be able to resist the enemy in the time of evil. Then after the battle you will still be standing firm. Stand your ground, putting on the belt of truth and the body armor of God's righteousness. For shoes, put on the peace that comes from the Good News so that you will be fully prepared. In addition to all of these, hold up the shield of faith to stop the fiery arrows of the evil one. Put on salvation as your helmet, and take the sword of the Spirit, which is the word of God. Pray in the Spirit at all times and on every occasion. Stay alert and be persistent in your prayers for all believers everywhere.

As a boy growing up, I was fascinated with the military and with how warfare works out between peoples. I was 12 at the time of our national bicentennial, and that sparked a growing love of history. And, perhaps sadly, warfare has been a main element of how events and differences are worked out between various nations. Toss it all together, add in the proverbial "East Coast US History trip" that my families took at this same time, and I thought being in the military might be a future. Our family has a long history of service, starting with my great-grandfather who fought for the Union army during the Civil War.

The idea of a war between God with his forces of light and an enemy (most often simply called "the Devil" or "Satan") along with the troops of darkness is throughout the Bible. God hides nothing from you. You are brought into this struggle as a ground soldier, or like I wrote earlier, maybe a secret agent who is infiltrating the enemy's territory in order to announce the good news to those people there. But, make no mistake, our enemy is not weak nor unaware of this struggle. You won't just be able to randomly enter into the territory of the enemy without proper preparation. Thus, this very famous passage from Ephesians that I learned at a very early age; over the years, I found more understanding as our work with Numinous continued.

The idea of a spiritual war is a vital aspect to grasp, before we look at the individual pieces of the armor. What God invites us into, as we saw when we looked at II Corinthians 5, is His work at reconciliation. That seems easy enough, right? Just go be salt and light in the world. We won't convince most people, but we live our lives in a way that points to God. But, as I suggested in the last chapter, there is another force at work in the world. We are told elsewhere that our enemy is like a lion, wandering about, looking for someone to devour. In the last book of the Bible, Revelation, we are given a description of the war between the enemy and our God, and there we are told that the enemy "declared war against...all who keep God's commandments and maintain their testimony for Jesus." (Rev 12)

I know the modern world doesn't like spiritual things, so they don't like the concept of a spiritual enemy. Though, in a funny way, many people also have a fascination with the idea as evidenced by the many movies, books and videos games that delve into the concept of an active evil spiritual being or beings. I guess they just don't like anything that could possibly hint to the veracity of the Bible's story. Regardless, it is vital for you to understand that having accepted Jesus, you are on his team. No matter what you may or may not think about the enemy, he is not unaware of you. Or, as Aragorn says to Theoden in *The Two Towers* movie, "open war is upon you whether you would risk it or not."

I don't mean to suggest that "The Devil" is coming for you personally. Nor that you somehow specifically are on his mind. There's probably more I should tell you on this, but for now, just realize that the enemy is far busier with more important issues or plans than you or I. We should not be afraid, nor should we somehow decide to blame the issues of our life "on Satan." Think of it more like a large-scale war. There is the leader of the two sides, and each has generals and various armies, on down to lower officers and rank basic soldiers. In the end, you might think of it like a world system, so in thinking that the system is always at work against your efforts...or more accurately, working against God's plan and since you are on God's team, well, you get involved in all of that.

We've talked at length about the need for your mind to be transformed. Well, this can be described as a battle within the mind. The concept of struggling to not think a certain way, or to avoid certain actions or beliefs...this is a large part of the war Paul is writing about in this passage. This writing comes at the end of Ephesians. Remember how I told you that Ephesians can be best understood as a little Christianity 101 type book? The last three chapters provide a basic understanding of what it means to be in a collective group of disciples together. I think Paul's writings there are the best and most clear explanation about how to "do church." So, after his prayer which concludes the personal salvation theology section, he dives into the "how should you live" section, covering a variety of topics. So, here he comes to the end of his planned writing; he starts the section by writing the word "finally."

Paul is basically saying "the last thing I want you to be aware of is that you are in a struggle with a real enemy." He lays out concepts about that first, and those verses have caused a variety of interpretations. Don't get lost there. Focus on the most important—you are in a conflict, and not with other humans. You aren't battling "flesh and blood." To survive this, you should make sure you enter that conflict prepared with the Lord's armor He has provided for you. You must wear the armor if you hope to resist the enemy. As many others have shown, all of the armor is defensive. This isn't really a call for you to "gear up" so you can go out and smack the enemy around. This isn't preparation for your hero moment. The armor is so you can be standing firm during and after the attack comes.

The pieces are then explained in an image that draws on the basic armor of a Roman soldier. When Paul writes this, the world superpower is the Roman Empire. Rome had grown from a tiny, weak city-state in the 500 BC era to become the dominate power by roughly 150BC when they defeated their main rival in Carthage. After that, the dominoes continued to fall as regional powers like the Gauls, the Celts and the Macedonians were defeated in battle. Paul knows the outfit for the Roman soldier very well, and he uses that imagery for description.

First the belt; why a belt? Without a belt, the rest of the clothing/armor does not stay on or not on well. You wouldn't want to be trying to stand firm in the struggle while also trying to keep everything in place. Truth does this for us. Realize that attacking the concept of "truth" has long been a strategy of the enemy, but this has grown more intense and direct over the past 30 years. You see this in how many openly state there is no absolute truth, or with flippant statements like something only being "true for you." If you lose truth, that nothing is every true independent of how one feels about it, understanding life in total is lost. Thus...truth is required

Then he talks about the body armor. You've seen enough movies to know that most blows from the opponent land on the body. The enemy is no different, and so Paul is reminding you that the only armor for these body blows is God's righteousness. Note that this isn't some demand that you become more righteous or that you be holy in yourself. Instead, we turn to God for Him to transform us, to mold us and make us more righteous. Take a look at Isaiah 59:17 for more context here to see how God prepares for battle

> *God put on righteousness as his body armor*
> *and placed the helmet of salvation on his head.*

Next you wear shoes. Seems obvious, but the connection here is about you bringing news of God's offered salvation to others. The picture of wearing shoes of the peace of that good news is evoking the same idea Paul wrote to the Roman church (Rom 10:15) where he asks who will go and take the good news to others? And if you are going, well you will be wearing shoes. Not surprising that Paul quotes Isaiah 52:7 that "how beautiful are the feet of the messenger who brings good news...of peace and salvation."

You will carry a shield. It is your faith, and Paul is clear to indicate that again you use it for defense. The enemy shoots arrows of fire at you. These arrows can be pain of experience where your faith will be needed to remind you to be content or that God is with you. The arrows may attack your provision, when you don't seem to have enough on which to live. You will feel frustration at life or may experience betrayal from a friend...the very kinds of things you might believe God should protect you from. You must hold tightly to your shield of faith in order to put out, to block those arrows. That the shield is "of faith" also hints that the enemy's attacks can be directly at your faith. There is his constant nagging of "how can you know God is there" and "are you sure God said that"? This is the sort of trick the enemy used against Eve and against Jesus, so don't be caught off guard when it comes at you.

Lastly, for the armor, we are to wear the helmet of salvation. Again, you've seen the many movies about battle and if the person isn't hit in the body, they are attacked at the head. Take off the helmet and soon enough you see that character taken out with a shot to the head. This should be easy for you to grasp because we've already talked at length about how the great battleground of your faith is in the mind.

I like how Paul wrote this same idea to the church at Thessalonica. In I Thessalonians 5:8, he tells them "let us who live in the light be clearheaded, protected by the armor of faith and love, and wearing as our helmet the confidence of our salvation." Tied to your faith, the mind is the place where you hold your confidence about what God has told you. Try to face the enemy without the helmet, and you'll quickly find yourself in doubt and wondering. Think about the passages that describe the mind: Rom 12:2; Eph 4:23; II Cor 10:5, Phil 4:8....we can keep our minds confident in the reality that we have been saved with our minds being transformed. OR, we can allow doubt to creep in and be conformed to the world's ways of thinking.

Finally, there is one weapon of attack described, the sword of the Spirit. And just in case we aren't following Paul well, he states openly that this means "the word of God." That is both the notion of God speaking to us, as He does, and also the written Bible. Cherish the Bible, girls. This is one reason I'm writing this for you. I want you to become interested even more deeply in God's word. We saw this identical concept of cherishing the Word of God when I showed you the verse in Psalm 119. Note also that the sword for the Roman soldier is the gladius, which is a short sword of maybe 2 feet. It is for hand-to-hand combat....so though the enemy can be shooting at us from far away (fiery darts), we will end up hand to hand, messy, pain, tribulation, trials, and suffering. Don't be surprised by this.

Finally, once armed, he gives direction for one action, one maneuver on the battlefield:

> *Pray in the Spirit at all times and on every occasion. Stay alert and be persistent in your prayers....*

Pray!

I haven't really spoken much about prayer through this book, so let me add here that as you are moving forward as a Christian disciple, you must constantly be communicating with God. Prayer is just that...talking to God. Not surprisingly, there are many books about prayer, so I won't belabor the point here, but there is also a lot of confusion regarding prayer. Or maybe better to say there is "a lot of complication" about how people think about prayer. Is it chanting? Is there a script? Is there a time limit? All of those things really miss the point which is that you want to further your relationship with God. As you hopefully know from your many friendships, the way to further a relationship is through communication. If you stop talking to people, the relationship dwindles. Choose to not engage with that person in life, the friendship will simply drift away.

When you talk to God, then, there are various things to talk about. Here, Paul is clearly speaking in regard to the battlefront. So, among the many things, you should be praying for God's protection. It is helpful to pray for Him to strengthen your guardian angels, and perhaps to send you more aid. Taking time to tell God the things you are thankful for, especially if the battle you face is connected to discouragement or issues of contentment. Of course the example Jesus gives us starts with worship ("Our Father, who art in heaven, hallowed be thy name"—"your name is to be celebrated, exalted, lifted high in worship"). Then, as you can see by Paul's second phrase, we should be praying for others. This act of intercession is going to God on behalf of another. You might ask Him for protection over them, strength during challenging times, patience in the face of life's issues, grace to sustain them through the dark valley or as we saw in Paul's prayer in this same letter, in Ephesians 3, to better understand love. I often pray for the person to hear God better or to sense His presence, to feel God's love surrounding them.

The command to "stay alert" is tied directly into prayer. I'm going to write more about this "alert" concept in another chapter, so for now just realize that the word for "watch" means "to keep awake or be on alert." Think about a guard on duty surrounding a campsite; we want that person to keep watchful. The idea in the Greek is very close to the concept to "have a sleepless night...do not sleep." The word "persistent" suggests constancy or perseverance, the idea of holding out, waiting, diligently staying at one's work.

As a disciple of God, there is a spiritual war going on around us. Don't be afraid. Don't run from this truth either. We already know Who has won the victory. Our God wins! We are simply asked to stay faithful for our time here on the planet. Yes, we may personally experience pain or, as I described last chapter, feel the loss of relationships, confront betrayal that will hurt. We may think our part has been a failure or insignificant. It is not. We get to participate in the greatest freedom campaign in all of world history. The enemy of our faith won't like it, and he will do all he can to oppose both you and the more general effort. He will lose.

Chapter 24

Colossians 3:12-15—Since God chose you to be the holy people he loves, you must clothe yourselves with tenderhearted mercy, kindness, humility, gentleness, and patience. Make allowance for each other's faults, and forgive anyone who offends you. Remember, the Lord forgave you, so you must forgive others. Above all, clothe yourselves with love, which binds us all together in perfect harmony. And let the peace that comes from Christ rule in your hearts. For as members of one body you are called to live in peace. And always be thankful.

Well, since I brought up the armor from Ephesians, I decided to give you the other half of the clothing of a Christian disciple. Think back to the description I just gave you about the armor. The need for the armor of God is for our daily goings out in the world, yet anyone who has studied armor even casually knows you don't just put that on over your skin.

This letter to the city of Colossae is actually a partner letter to what you read in Ephesians. It's a shorter version of the same concept...a primer in basic Christianity. Here, I think Paul gives us the necessary companion clothing to go with the armor. Of course, this idea isn't in the text per se, but since these two letters are considered twins or sister-letters, and in both, Paul talks about what we should wear as a disciple, I think my idea has merit.   Instead of just thinking about each day as a battlefield where one must wear armor, a battle image that can actually be taken too far, I think Paul is reminding us that our armor rests on equally important concepts that are relational in spirit.

You hopefully can see this image easily.   Paul describes eight pieces of clothing to put on for your daily encounters with other people, especially with other Christians. If every Christian would wear these pieces of clothing, the world would be a much better place. Below I will first use the word from the verse and then give you other ideas from the Greek:

- Tenderhearted mercy can be understood as a heart of compassion, meaning that in your most inner spirit you have a seat of emotions and from there, you act and think in terms of compassion to others
- Kindness is sometimes the throwaway idea, as if being "kind" is something only the weak do, and yet it is not. The Greek word also suggests goodness or generosity; not really in financial matters, but more of a generous spirit in which you do or give kind acts to another.
- Humility is tied to the notion of lowliness in one's thinking. We've seen this expressed in the Romans 12:3 verse, to not think more highly of oneself.   Or the Philippians 2 passage to think first, or think more, about others. We recognize that God is the only one worthy of a claim to honor or position.
- Gentleness is not just the idea of softness, as in "she was so gentle with the baby." It also includes the concept of meekness, courtesy or even being considerate.   This would include the idea that because of your faith in God,

you can remain gentle even in the face of opposition or hateful things done to you.

- Patience, or the older term of longsuffering, speaks to one withholding action or comment rather than rushing in. This piece of clothing will quietly stand under attack or an injustice done to you. You are holding tightly to His ways regardless of your circumstances knowing that in the end, God wins and everything will make sense.

- Make allowance (for each other's faults) is really the thought of enduring or putting up with someone's actions. The Greek verb tense would suggest that this is done continually, never ending.

- Forgive anyone; in the Greek word, the concept is forgiveness with grace. Here, you are giving this gift of forgiveness freely, with no strings attached. Behind this, Paul makes clear that the point is to clearly mimic Jesus. God has freely given you forgiveness thus so should you to anyone else.

- Finally, Paul closes his list with love; above all else clothe yourself with love. The Greek is again the word agape, the sacrificial love that gives to another regardless of the situation, regardless of the relationship. This virtue being shown as superior shouldn't surprise you as you think back on our conversation surrounding the John 13 passage or the list from Galatians 5. Throughout the Bible, love is shown as the primary expression of relationship (review I Corinthians 13)

So, what does all of this mean for us? Well, these "items of clothing" are the first thing a Christian should be known for. You put on the clothing before you put on the armor. Here I put on the clothes of mercy, kindness, humility, gentleness, patience and love. Then, after I have those clothes on, I can then put on the Ephesians six armor...ready for the day.

While I just wrote you last chapter that we are in a war, it is vital for you to not miss Paul's warning in the Ephesians passage that we are NOT in a war with other humans. Some take the armor passage as license to go into battle, usually verbal, with other people. That is actually harmful to the mission of God. No one will accept an offer to be reconciled with God coming from someone yelling at them.

You can see how Paul thinks about this relationally with other humans by the last verse of this passage where he says that as you wear these items of clothing, peace with others should rule over you and your actions. "You are called to live in peace."

He deepens this point about relationship in the subsequent verses, especially the exhortation that whatever you do or whatever you say to another person, do it as the representative of Jesus. Have you ever represented another person? Maybe not in your young lives, but you will soon enough. As you do that, you must keep in mind that, in that moment, you are no long really "you", but you are standing there as the representation of the other person or organization. You should always be thinking "I need to make sure I don't do anything to bring dishonor or embarrassment on the person I am representing."

Yes, there is a struggle with a real enemy that opposes everything God stands for, and he will see you as a part of God's team, and thus also oppose you. You, though, walk in the world in this clothing of love and mercy and caring, modeling peace and thankfulness before all other people. You do have on the armor of God, ready to defend your own spiritual journey as you find yourself opposed by our enemy and his actions, but through it all you are moving in the world in a way that all can see and sense this clothing.

Chapter 25

II Corinthians 10:3-5—For though we live as human beings, we do not wage war according to human standards, for the weapons of our warfare are not human weapons, but are made powerful by God for tearing down strongholds. We tear down arguments and every arrogant obstacle is raised up against the knowledge of God, and we take every thought captive to make it obey Christ.

Since the last two verses I have discussed with you were about warfare and how we are to clothe ourselves for daily life, I wanted to share this verse from Paul's second letter to the church in Corinth. I first told you about this verse when we looked at Romans 12:2; there I first told you about the necessity of allowing God to transform your mind. Over the past two decades, this reality that the battle is in the mind has been made more clear. It's not that we do not operate in the real world nor that we don't confront other battlefields such as our actions or pursuing justice in life, however everything starts internally.

Here, Paul is presenting this truth to the church in Corinth because they have been impacted by a deviant theology. They are being taught a different gospel than that of the apostles who first brought them the truth about Jesus. Paul is responding to a philosophical or mental attack on the church; that attack is aimed at how we live. So, at this point in his letter he starts to defend what the apostles had laid out as the theology of Jesus.

As he describes it, he produces another metaphor for battle, talking about weapons. This is why I like this verse tied to the passages in Ephesians 6 and Colossians 3. We know from those passages that each day we enter the world and how we "dress for the day" is vital. We first put on the clothing of virtues, as expressed in Colossians 3; then we put on the defensive armor of God laid out in Ephesians 6. Here, Paul mentions weapons in plural, even though in Ephesians the only weapon is the Sword of the Spirit. I think he is implying that prayer is used as a weapon, much like he suggested in Ephesians where he said the main action of the soldier is to pray ("take your stand and pray").

Of course, to see prayer as a weapon might not be the best picture or even accurate...we aren't using prayer in some manner to "attack." And remember, we certainly are not attacking other humans. Paul is explicit in Ephesians on that point, and I think he alludes to it here in II Corinthians. He states that we don't war or fight as the world does, not as humans will; we also do not use human weapons, as one might expect. In other words, all of the struggle is not against a human but against spiritual issues and, as Paul means here, against mental or philosophical issues. Thus, back to the battle in the mind.

The war, and especially the reason for the armor, is to win that mental struggle. As we saw with Romans 12:2, this involves surrender allowing God to transform the mind. That transformation is not something we have the ability to do ourselves. Yet, at the same time, there is an action involved that we must perform. It is the active decision to guard your mind and be aware of your own thoughts. At the same time, part of the action of spiritual warfare is becoming aware about the ideas or concepts that are being presented to you by others.

When Paul talks about "strongholds," he is referencing the concept of being confronted by false ideas. This word can be understood as a castle or a fortress. Hopefully you remember the various times we've visited such a place. The closest one to us is the fort in St. Augustine. Remember going there? It is huge with thick walls, right? No army could easily take the fortress, nor could just any weapon destroy the walls.

In our modern world, ideas and concepts are among the toughest "things" to take down. Once you determine that a thought or philosophy is right or true, well, it is hard to move away from it. As I often tell my students, each person believes what they believe strongly--"you hold your beliefs dearly bought." No one just randomly has a belief. I hope then you can see how such a thought becomes a stronghold. Each of you has certain things that you believe deeply, and you protect it. Some of our beliefs are insignificant—you all know how I feel about Coke and Pepsi...it's a stronghold for sure (Coke is the only drink for me), but it's not significant thing either way. Same about my love of the Dodgers or my disdain for the University of Alabama. But other thoughts are significant such as your view on truth or on personhood or on justice; again, once a person adopts a viewpoint it is nigh impossible for them to change.

What if that thought is erroneous? This is where Paul is coming from. He believes that the church at Corinth is being infected with wrong thinking, wrong ideas...strongholds. So, he knows that he has a weapon to take against that...the truth of God's word. In that act of bringing truth, he then gives one of my favorite phrases:

we take every thought captive

Now, most likely, in the context of the passage, Paul is mostly thinking about capturing these false ideas or notions that are being suggested to the church in Corinth. And, as he says, by taking them the obedience of Christ, they are destroyed.

I have always added to this though, or not really added, but just livened up the image. As Paul says, we are taking this captured thought to Jesus sitting on his throne. So, I confront a thought and take it captive….then, I take that captive thought to God's throne so that He can judge it. He does, and by doing so, informs me. In other words, rather than me deciding the truth or veracity of a thought, I just take it captive and present it to Jesus on His throne. There, by using God's word, He shows me whether the idea or philosophy is true or false. This is vitally important as we make our way through life. There are many ideas that come at us, sometimes from friends, perhaps through school, or we watch something through media. An idea could sound rather nice or fair or good…but we don't actually know. We are not God. We need the Judge to review the idea and instruct us what to do with it.

I think you can even press this image further as a method by which we participate in the transformation of the mind. What I mean is that rather than seeing this verse only in the context of the larger church issue that Paul is confronting in Corinth, I can also realize that any thought I have can be, even should be, taken captive. Think back again to the ideas of Romans 12:2…since I know that I need my mind to be transformed, AND I need to avoid being conformed by the world's way of thinking….here is a way to do that. I take every thought captive. I don't allow these thoughts to land at all in my mind without a rigorous examination. Again, I stress, not an examination by my own self---I can't trust myself to necessarily see past any deceptions—no, instead I take these thoughts to God's throne in order for HIM to teach me.

The idea of capturing our thoughts, as Paul describes the battle in the mind, is certainly the struggle with human reasoning and false arguments, but this is also vital in dealing with our own internal mental struggles. Think about this as a tool to deal with our own negative self-talk. Maybe I think that "I'm a loser." Or, I worry that "God doesn't like me." Maybe I think "my life is not really abundant." If I sit on those false thoughts, I can begin to spiral downwards into negativity. I can beat myself up, and really, this is an act of war by the enemy. He hints to me with lies and I listen. I let that thought just slide into my mind and begin to impact my feelings in that moment. Instead, what Paul says here is that I have agency. I can decide to guard my mind in a way to where I capture each thought and take it to God's throne for cross-examination.

So, the discipline of taking this action of war, to capture these thoughts, is vital to succeeding in allowing God to transform my mind. When that happens, I am fixing, setting, focusing my mind. I am being aware of the thoughts around me. I am, in one sense, acting in the "third person." I am watching myself think, watching myself view concepts, being aware of the images and ideas in front of me. None of them are to be trusted---not from the media, not from Pastors, not from advertising, not from Christian singers, and not from my friends. I take captive EVERY thought. I fix my mind.

That concept of fixing the mind, focusing the mind, brings up two other wonderful passages that fit well here that help us with the final piece of this action. Both are, yet again, about the battle in the mind and showing us how God transforms our thinking. In his letters to Colosse and Philippi, Paul states this same "fix your mind" concept.

Colossians 3:2—Fix your minds on things above, not on earthly things

Philippians 4:8—Fix your thoughts on what is true, and honorable, and right, and pure, and lovely, and admirable. Think about things that are excellent and worthy of praise.

See it? Martin Luther, in teaching about dealing with sin and habits, said that "you can't stop the birds from flying over your head, but you can stop them from nesting in your hair." You won't be able to stop or control the thoughts or ideas swirling around you. You can, however, take action to stop or control any thoughts from building a stronghold in your mind.

Taking captive those thoughts, negative or proud or pretensive thoughts, is not good enough. We must replace those thoughts by fixing our mind on something else. Both of these verses show us what to do. Fix your mind (there's that verb of action, taking agency) on things above. Paul urges us to fill the mind with thoughts that are true, honorable, right, purer, lovely and admirable. Excellent and worthy of praise things also fit the bill.

We must take captive the wrong thoughts and instead, replace those prideful thoughts with thinking about these good thoughts, ideas and things worthy of praise. When we do that, we are engaging the life journey that was described for us in Psalm 1, where our mind is focused on God. Don't you just love that? God doesn't simply say "quit thinking about certain" things, but rather instructs us how to replace those thoughts with the right images and ideas.

Chapter 26

Romans 8:31—What shall we say about such wonderful things as these? If God is for us, who can ever be against us?

Earlier in the book, I shared with you God's command to us to be courageous in the face of challenges. Do you remember the "why"? It was because God said He would be with us wherever we would go. In Paul's letter to the church at Rome, he brings up this exact same point in what is one of the most famous chapters in all of the Bible. After three verses that talk about the spiritual battle we face in life, I wanted to point you back to this crucial Christian idea by sharing these verses that I've known as a boy.

Paul's letter to the Romans is considered by many the deepest theological writing of the New Testament. Paul certainly spent more time here than in most of his other letters. In the first seven chapters, he describes the saving work of Jesus for each of us. Along the way, he is taking pains to show how the life of faith that Jesus calls us to is free of the old laws that the Jewish people had followed. Jesus hadn't abandoned the law as worthless, but rather fulfilled those laws in a deeper way, calling each of us to follow in this new covenant relationship.

Reaching chapter 8, Paul lays out verses of promise and encouragement that is one of the most beautiful in the Bible. There's so much there that one could write an entire book just on this chapter. He talks about the freedom of Jesus, freedom from religious rules created by humans. He shares about prayer, about waiting, about being chosen by God, about hope, and how God is constantly working for our good.

As he reaches the conclusion, Paul begins with our focus verse. Hopefully it sparks for you the Joshua 1:9 verse. God is for us. Remember the name for Jesus—Immanuel. God with us. As He walks with us, inhabits life with you through the Holy Spirit, Paul states the obvious:

Who can ever be against us?

When we read about war, about wearing armor or having to constantly be on guard, it's easy to get nervous or afraid. No one really wants to get into conflict with others, and certainly if you tell me the struggle is with some spiritual powerful being…my goodness, I don't want to face that.

Similarly, as we walk daily with the Father, living life with His rules and guidance, others can bring condemnation or accusation against us. They can criticize and critique what we do and what we say. So even though I remember that the war is not "against flesh and blood," sometimes it sure feels like someone of "flesh and blood" is attacking me. In these moments, Paul wants to ensure that you and I never lose sight of the fact that God is for us! He loves us deeply. That fact is demonstrated by the fact that God sacrificed His own son for us.

Paul really starts rolling at this point in chapter eight. Since it is clear that God has chosen us as a valuable possession, then who dares accuse us of some failure. In other words, someone may come along and suggest that you have not accomplished some religious ritual properly. You may get accused of not worshipping the correct way. Those accusations are empty, we can say in retort, because the God of the Universe has chosen us for His own. No one may accuse us. No one may condemn us.

Wow!! That is so good.

It gets better!

Since we know that God is for us, and we have been chosen by Him, what does that mean but the obvious fact that He loves us. So, Paul digs into that idea with another rhetorical question...who can separate us from that love? Clearly no created being can. There is only one eternal Being, God; all others including our spiritual enemy are created, not eternal. There is no being of any type who can separate us from God's love for us.

Now, Paul wants to make sure you understand that the challenges of life are not evidence against God's love. Paul writes "Does it mean he no longer loves us if we have trouble or calamity, or are persecuted, or hungry, or destitute, or in danger, or threatened with death?" As we have noted throughout this book as we examine all these different verses, we will have challenges. For many who approach the Christian faith, they struggle to grasp this point.

In the minds of many, they see only two choices, especially if we start with the premise of God's great power and that He is with us. They think that the Christian faith, along with its promises of "life abundant" or that whatever we do "will prosper," suggests that God will keep us from all of life's issues. So, if I confront pain or lack, then it must mean God doesn't love me or is not with me. Or, they think, if they do experience the hard moments of life such as persecution or not having enough to eat or money problems, then this is evidence that there is no God (or, maybe that God is a Being far away in space who cares little for the human).

We have now tiptoed into the theological conundrum of "the problem of pain." As that's not really the point of the book, I'm going to leave the depths of that point to the side. If you want more, go read C.S. Lewis' masterful work entitled *The Problem of Pain*. Do note, however, that as I have shared elsewhere in this book, we are not the equal of God. We cannot fully comprehend His plans or strategies. As such, it is completely logical to say that we have been given, are living, a life of abundance, full of grace and His love and yet also have hard times and issues. Or, as Paul is saying here, it is true that we often confront these issues of trouble or calamity, but the fact of that does not in any way mean that God has left us or that He no longer loves us. In fact, as Paul notes, regardless of all these things, "overwhelming victory" is ours.

Overwhelming victory!

Now, Paul keeps going. See what I mean about this being a delicious chapter of God's truth? So, the issues of life can still happen to us, but God still loves us. Yet...is it possible for some external factor or power to remove us from God's love? So, Paul concludes the chapter with this powerful declaration.

I am convinced that nothing can ever separate us from God's love.

Read it again. NOTHING. CAN. EVER. SEPARATE.

If you want a verse to meditate on, this would be a good choice. Just chew on that for a while. Take a walk and keep repeating that idea. Turn it over in your mind. What can separate you? Nothing. What about for a short time? Nope.

My prayer for you is that you will live openly and deeply in this truth. You can rest in assurance that God is for you. Again, it's very similar to what God told Joshua. Wherever you go, God is with you. Whatever you confront, God loves you. In the midst of isolation, He is there. When under tremendous pressure from the world's challenges such as a health crisis or a financial downturn, He still loves you. That you are facing trials and tribulations are no evidence that somehow you have failed God or that He is mad at you. Look at Psalm 56:4 to see this same promise: I trust in God, so why should I be afraid? What can mere mortals do to me?

So, as you go through life, keep this verse firmly implanted in your mind. Since God is with you, who or what can ever be against you? Quiet confidence. Confident and courageous, just as prayed over you night after night, year after year.

Chapter 27

Micah 6:6-8—What can we bring to the Lord? Should we bring him burnt offerings? Should we bow before God Most High with offerings of yearling calves? Should we offer him thousands of rams and ten thousand rivers of olive oil? Should we sacrifice our firstborn children to pay for our sins? No, O people, the Lord has told you what is good, and this is what he requires of you: to do what is right, to love mercy, and to walk humbly with your God.

Hosea 6:6—I want you to show love, not offer sacrifices. I want you to know me more than I want burnt offerings.

Zechariah 7:9-10—This is what the Lord of Heaven's Armies says: Judge fairly, and show mercy and kindness to one another. Do not oppress widows, orphans, foreigners, and the poor. And do not scheme against each other.

As the years went along in our journey with Numinous and you girls entered your young child years, these verses began to become more important to me. One of the key things that I tried to teach our members was what it meant to walk successfully with God. Now the idea of "success" gets turned on its head in God's kingdom, as we have seen. This is not the world's view of accomplishments, wealth or power. There is no accumulation for self in this concept.

We've talked at length in this book about the notion of how so much depends on our thoughts. That's where the path to success begins. Allowing God to transform your thinking. However, it doesn't merely stay there. The idea from Luke 9 about sacrificing daily and taking up your cross, or the concept we saw about the mission for the Christian of being active in the ministry of reconciliation, being salt and light, are not private or secretive things. They are not only in the mind, so to speak. Rather, it is our engagement with the world.

As another verse says well, we are not of the world, but we are in the world. We are living here. God loves each person alive on the planet. He also loves the planet as His creation. God wants His children active in the world. We are engaged in an attempt to make it better. Of course, we must realize that the enemy of God is also the enemy of the world, and we will not, on our own, make it fully better. We humans will never create utopia on earth. That we wish to create a "best" is evidence of the subconscious calling back to the Garden...but we will not create a new Garden of Eden on our own. However, rather than retreating in sadness thinking it's all pointless, we instead look with hope towards a future whose end we already know. God wins! The world does get redeemed.

So that leads us to this trifecta of verses. As I hope you can see, there is a theme running between them. All three, if you read the other verses around them, give us a picture of God telling His people how He wants them to act. He is very clear that whatever they think worship of Him looks like, they are getting it wrong. All three prophecies chastise the reader for thinking only in terms of holy acts like singing or fasting. In spots we could even say God is mocking these people for all their religious efforts all the while missing what He thinks is core.

This is obviously a hard thing for us humans to get because I'm sure you notice around you that we have the same problem in these days. Hosea was writing around the 760s BC and Micah wrote a few years later, in the 730s, both before the two kingdoms were destroyed. Assyria actually does destroy the northern kingdom in the 720s, right after these warnings; obviously, the people did not listen.

Zechariah shows us that even after the punishment from Assyria and Babylon, the people were still not listening. He writes around the 520s BC and yet you can tell he's got the same message. In fact, in v7, he points out that their actions, and thus subsequent failure to do the worship acts that God wants, is "the same message the Lord proclaimed through the prophets...." Later, in v.11, he is stronger, saying "Your ancestors stubbornly refused to listen to this message...they made their hearts as hard as stone, so they could not hear the instructions...the Lord...had sent them."

Isn't that tragic? I mean, you get a warning, but fail to listen. Thus, punishment comes. After the punishment is over, so now we can back to living well. Right? Well, nope, because for some reason, you just go right back to the same errors as before. If I didn't know this describes my own life, I would be more critical. Clearly, we humans have an issue to where we don't pay attention to what God wants.

Note, this criticism of spiritual activity is not to say that God doesn't want us to sing or doesn't want us to fast or pray. He does. He makes that clear elsewhere. You should honor God by giving a portion of your money or possessions to Him. You should have holy celebrations like Easter or Christmas. However, when God looks around and sees general oppression among His people and in the world, those songs or acts become meaningless.

God is justice. He is mercy. He is a Father to the fatherless. He is there for the widow. He is there for the oppressed. He is the "God who sees you."

You might wonder, "well why doesn't He do something?" He would reply that He has...first through Jesus, but from there, in each of you. Remember what we saw in the II Corinthians 5 passage? We are on mission for God in the ministry of reconciliation. You, if you are a believer, are God's hands and feet. He is looking at us to see that we are acting as the one who brings His peace, His justice to others. His retort to the above question would be "why aren't YOU doing something, person of faith." Hence these verses.

Notice how all three bring this consistent theme. Micah talks about justice ("do what is right"), mercy (kindness) and humility. Hosea talks about love (in the Greek version from the latter BC years, they translated it as mercy); you can translate the Hebrew into loyalty or faithfulness to the covenant. Zechariah again brings out justice ("judge fairly"), mercy and kindness. He also points out that oppression is not to be done, whether to the weak stranger or to someone you know within the community.

Do not oppress widows, orphans, foreigners, and the poor. And do not scheme against each other.

I hope you can see how clear this is. There is no secret, no hidden agenda. You don't have to wonder about what actions to take in your life. You simply have to be intentional. Far too often Christians had supposed that they were in the clear here, and yet upon examination it was clear that the person had, well, failed to examine their own actions with detail. As you hopefully know, the failure to act is as bad as an action itself. You may not personally be involved in oppression or bullying (I certainly hope not; you know how much I abhor bullying in particular), but if it is going on around you and you don't act, then to God, you are involved.

This can happen in your purchasing. Take the time to do all you can to investigate what you buy, and from where. Acts of injustice can come from your media content. Refuse to give any support to movies, books or movies that promote or highlight oppressive acts. We can fail to act as God demands in whom you continue to be friends with. If you see a companion acting in a way that isn't about justice or mercy or kindness, then you should approach them on the point. If they won't change, then it is time for you to move on in the relationship.

And, on the other side, seek out companies and media and friends who DO support humility, justice, mercy, kindness...especially those that aim to step into the gap within our society. No, you can't fix how a business treats its workers, say with low pay, but you can give financial support to ministries and aid agencies that seek to help with finances or perhaps legal aid.

It is vital, my dear children, that you move beyond the simple verbal acknowledgment of your faith, and into letting your light shine before all in the actions of your life. That wonderful children's song holds much truth. And yes, letting your light shine does involve, for instance, reading your Bible (maybe even openly) and certainly speaking openly about your faith. As I showed you back in the chapter on Galatians 6:14, "as for me, may I never boast about anything except the cross of our Lord Jesus Christ." So, I will boast in Him; I will speak out to others about the glory of God and the mercy of His son. Yet, if all we have are these words, then we become like the listeners of these prophets from 100s of years ago...a people more determined to perform the acts of worship than engaging in the work of justice and mercy.

And that work, justice and mercy...that is the kind of worship God wants from us.

Chapter 28

I Peter 5:8--Be Sober! Stay alert and awake!!

1:13 Therefore, get your minds ready for action by being fully sober, and set your hope completely on the grace that will be brought to you when Jesus Christ is revealed.

4:7 For the culmination of all things is near. So be self-controlled and sober-minded for the sake of prayer.

5:8 Be sober and alert. Your enemy the devil, like a roaring lion, is on the prowl looking for someone to devour.

Around 2015, as you hopefully remember since you were there, we brought our journey with Numinous to a close. We felt God's leadership telling us to bring our ship into port and release all those still with us. I mention that in order to set the context for the last few verses that I wish to share with you. I am now in my 50s, and this change regarding Numinous has become a key part of my life experience in this fifth decade. That change, both with Numinous and my age, did not diminish my need and hunger to read God's word. So, I kept my study of the Word even though I wasn't preparing to preach to anyone.

I urge you girls to remain hungry for His truth. Even after 56 years, and probably about 45 years after I first read the Bible through, I still turn to His Word. And, wonderfully, He meets me there to still instruct me. Every time I study the Bible, new ideas will come to me through the verses I am reading. Even though I've read the verses multiple times, I will see something fresh. That's what happened to me when I was taking time to study Peter's first letter in-depth.

Peter was writing to some of the earliest churches that had been born during Paul's first missionary trips. Peter was writing around 60 AD, so roughly 30 years after Jesus had ascended; this is the same time that Paul was writing to the church at Ephesus and Philippi. These were the years when Nero was Emperor of Rome, and through him, intense persecution was coming to Christians. This idea of understanding that challenging times are to be assumed by the follower of Jesus is, as we have seen, not unusual. Yet, Peter wanted to help remind his readers that they must be mentally prepared.

He uses the same word in the writing to express this: sober. That may not seem like a big deal, but that vocabulary word was used only six times in the entire New Testament...so half of those moments come from Peter here. He wanted to stress a specific notion of mental alertness. I was reading and studying this letter in the spring of 2018, and Peter's intensity really captured me as our own nation was experiencing challenging times. The idea was so vivid that these verses (particularly 5:8) became one of my newest focus verses....and hence now I am showing it to you.

In the Greek, verse 8 starts off with just two words. In English, it would be commands.

Be Sober! Stay alert!!

Why? Because, as we have seen elsewhere, there is an enemy. And that enemy is not passive, not merely biding time. Instead, he is prowling much like a great lion seeking someone to devour. The context of this verse is interesting because immediately before, Peter had just suggested the Christian could relax. He writes we should "cast all our cares" on God. In other words, "don't worry; be happy." The word picture in verse seven is of tossing your bags upon a beast of burden, like a mule. We might think of it as placing our luggage on a moving sidewalk or those moving platforms in the airport where our luggage gets whisked into the back, heading for the plane. No human has to lift a finger, at least not for a while.

Peter is saying that we can release carrying the baggage of worries or cares, and instead place them on God. God will carry them for us. Well, think about how one often feels when you give up your luggage or stepping onto a moving sidewalk. You relax. You are in the airport, and now someone else is managing your heavy bag. You can simply stroll along with no worries to the gate. This is, of course, a good thing. It flows out of what we've looked at in the Joshua and Romans 8 passage. God is for us! He is with us, even to the point of carrying our cares.

But then Peter pounces with a seemingly paradoxical idea of verse 8. It's almost like you can hear him saying "HOWEVER...don't let your guard down." In other words, even as you give your worries to God, you must stay mentally alert! You cannot relax your guard. He might even have been thinking of what Paul was writing to Ephesus about wearing the armor of God. Peter is saying you are in a battle; there is danger around.

Your enemy is strong, vicious and not casual about efforts. The command of "stay alert" can also be translated as "stay awake." You can't be on guard if you are sleepy.

In the previous chapter, Peter used this same word to give the context to his readers that this struggle is a part of the "end times." It might be hard to believe that he would write such in 60 AD. Now nearly 2000 years later, many other people have wondered if their own days are the same "end times." Perhaps all of the post-ascension years should be considered "end times." Clearly Peter was not writing his audience about some far distant future. It was vital, in Peter's thought, in those years of Nero, to be conscious of the struggle.

Notice how, in chapter four, he also places the action of the "fighting Christian" as prayer. We saw this same idea from Paul when we studied the "armor of God" passage in Ephesians. So, in I Peter 4:7, the command of "be sober" is paired with having a "sound mind." Some translators will use "sober" there too, almost to double up the punch: "be sober minded and be sober." Note, none of this is suggesting a connection to alcohol; it is all about alertness in your mind.

All three passages are like this. As we saw in chapter 5, though "mind" is not mentioned specifically there, clearly Peter is saying that you must be mentally alert, awake and sober. The idea of "be sober", in these three distinct places, denotes self-control and clarity of mind. This should remind you of the many passages we've looked at already that describe the necessity for mental clarity. "Be not conformed [in your mind] but rather be transformed through the renewing of your mind."

Peter starts out the entire letter with this concept when he first mentions soberness. He urges his readers to get ready for action; "gird up your loins" is a very old term which connects to the idea of running in a robe. Since that is very difficult (think of running in a long dress), the only way to really do it is to pull up the flowing portion, holding it up or tucking it into a belt so that your legs are exposed, like with shorts. Then, you can run.

So, he starts that verse in chapter one that way...get ready to run in your life. How? In your mind. Prepare your mind for action, for movement, for the flow of living that ebbs and flows constantly. How do we do that? Be sober minded. There it is again.

The summary could be understood this way with all three passages. In chapter one, be well balanced and have self-control in your sober mind with your hope set on Jesus. In chapter four, have self-restraint, be sober, keep a clear head, to help in your prayers. Finally, in chapter five, stay alert, awake and sober in your mind, be self-possessed, in all circumstances especially knowing that you are on a battleground with a ruthless enemy.

The call to mental alertness has, I think, been brought more to the surface now when I write this in the middle of the coronavirus pandemic. We've just passed day 200 since all of that started back in March 2020, at least here in the USA. Having spent most of those days sitting at my computer, in isolation, the mind quickly can drift, become distracted or overly dull. There is also a lot of overall conflict in these days which makes it challenging for the believer to know where to stand and what causes to take up. In days like these, soberness of mind is critical.

To walk well on your journey, you must be mentally alert for what life throws at you. Only in such soberness of mind are you ready to step into acts of justice or fulfill the mission of being God's ambassador. This is the life of the Christian disciple walking with the light of God shining clearly the way forward.

Chapter 29

Hebrews 12:12-13—So take a new grip with your tired hands and strengthen your weak knees. Mark out a straight path for your feet so that those who are weak and lame will not fall but become strong.

If there is any lesson that becomes more clear as you age, it is that the journey of faith is indeed hard. Of course, I think most, Christian or not, would agree that the older they get, the more pain there is. Sometimes it is emotional. Other times it is due to loss of friends or close relatives. You can experience financial challenge or medical issues. In general, the body starts to break down.

I wrote about this in one of my songs when I turned 40...now over 16 years ago

> *I'm aging faster now, my heart's more broken now.*
> *I think the warranty's out. I think the parts are breaking down.*

For the Christian, though, there is another level of challenge. The disciple wants to see God's Kingdom come. They want to see people get saved. They want justice and holiness to rise in the culture. Yet, as we have established, there is an enemy who, for now, seems to consistently have the upper hand. That passion of the faithful believer to bring about good crashes headlong into opposition the world seek solutions that are counter to God. People say they want peace, but as Jesus told us, the peace He brings is not what the world expects. People want justice, but typically in a way that ultimately can bring pain and suffering to others. We humans simply don't know how to do holy living, which of course is why we need the Holy Spirit consistently transforming us in our mind and in how we live.

The writer of Hebrews is focused on maintaining our faith in the midst of challenging times. Biblical experts are not sure exactly who wrote the book nor when, but the general consensus about the timing places it near the same moment when Peter wrote. Its still that same time when Nero was Emperor and persecution for the faithful had emerged. Not only was there external oppression, internally the faith was going through difficulty as variations of Jesus' message, as well as who He really was, had caused division.

Much like today, to stand firm in the historic message of Jesus was challenging. Many, in and out of the faith, demand accommodation with culture. If you really speak authentically for the Christian message, you can be accused of being hateful. Your efforts to bring truth about peace might be labeled as causing strife. Again, Jesus warned of us this, and that is part of what the author is trying to say here.

This verse stands at the end of a section that begins in chapter 10. The writer had been, in the previous chapters, defending the authority of Jesus as our High Priest and the perfect sacrifice for our faith. The author had warned about departing from the true faith. Then in vv 10:19-25, he launches into an exhortation to remaining faithful in challenging times. In v 35, he says "don't throw away this confident trust in the Lord...patient endurance is what you need now."

Then, in what is perhaps the most stirring chapter in the New Testament, he recounts the various stories from the Bible in which these people from history stood strong in faith. Their faith wasn't in peaceful or easy times, but rather through challenge, suffering and hardship. You should read that chapter, the famous "Roll Call of Faith" in Hebrews 11...and perhaps read it often to let your own faith and spark of life be rekindled. God is not weary. His plans are not thwarted nor is He surprised by things going on in the world.

So, into chapter 12 we go. We are urged to "run with endurance the race God has set before" you. To help us, the writer points out just how much more suffering Jesus endured. Remember, as was just pointed out, Jesus is the perfect sacrifice, our model, our healer, and yet He too suffered. These words are not a dig at us, like "your supposed pain is nothing." No...the writer knows we are struggling and weary. He realizes that it is far easier to give up, to quit. Or, to quote another song, this time by Steve Taylor--who himself is quoting Flannery O'Conner from her book *The Habit of Being*--"it's harder to believe than not to." Or you hopefully remember reading this quote from G. K. Chesterton that I have in my email signature: "The Christian ideal has not been tried and found wanting. It has been found difficult and left untried."

So, the writer urges us in v.3 to think about Jesus and what he endured so that you "won't become weary and give up." Make sure you see his context...he is talking mostly about confronting the challenges that are "external to your person," what he has just spent the last 2 chapters writing about. But then, he quickly adds another concept in vv.5-11 to remind us that our "suffering" can come internally.

We can choose to sin, to act in ways that are not in keeping with God's way. When that happens, God steps in as a loving Father to discipline us. I am confident that each of you remember the times when Mom and I had to discipline you. We used a variety of ways that morphed as you aged, appropriate for the moment, but in a way that grabbed your attention. We had specific and certain ways we wanted you to learn to act, whether towards each other or in how you talked or in choices that you made. It is the specific task of parents to help mold a child, and as Christians, to mold that child in God's ways. No human follows the path of God just on their own desire; instead like an athlete or artist, we have to be trained. That training, that discipline, is never fun...whether we mean the idea of discipline as "pain caused to bring a change of behavior" or we mean the idea of discipline as "a determined set action one does repeatedly, a habit of action."

God is a loving Father. When I sin, He disciplines me. When I think wrongly, He admonishes that thought and brings me back to truth. When I act or speak inappropriately, He uses various tools to cause me to change my behavior and words. No...it's not fun, but in the end, this coaching pays off to bring a "harvest of right living."

So, keeping both aspects related to suffering in balance, that our suffering can be external, done "to us" or can be internal, "brought on by my actions," the author drops this beautiful nugget of wisdom.

I don't fully remember when God first showed this to me, but I know it was in these last years of Numinous. In the years before we finally heard His directive to shut down, I was so weary. The initial enthusiasm of many others had dissipated. Some had moved away, others had simply faded away out of the group. Even those who were faithfully on the journey with us had seemingly become consumed with many other things of life. I felt alone. Even your blessed mother had, as you know, started back to school to pursue her dream of becoming a nurse. That was a decision we made together, one I know was completely right, and yet as far as the ministry went, it left me feeling increasingly isolated.

In that time, when I was so tired, feeling so discouraged that my efforts in ministry were pointless, effecting little change, He brought me to this verse. The message is clear. NEVER GIVE UP! I just love how this comes out much like a trainer or coach would say (yell?) at us:

...take a new grip! Strengthen your weak knees!

Walk straight on the path! And look, doing so is not just for yourself, but for others. That's good stuff! You girls remember I was a swim coach before you were born. I said these kinds of exhorting statements to my swimmers. Keep going! Push! Strive! You can do it! Suck it up! Focus!!

You probably see the connection between this verse and the last one I showed you from I Peter. Stay alert. Don't lose your way. Be sober minded at all times. Whether due to external persecution or confronting your own sins, be strong in your endurance. Note that there is no suggestion that your feelings are false. He doesn't write "quit moaning about supposedly being tired; you aren't tired." No. God understands that you are tired. Your knees are weak. But then, in the midst of that, He comes to you urging you to do something about this. Take a new grip!

Have you lifted weights? I know you've carried things. Remember moving a sofa when you moved apartments? As you carry it, you can feel it starting to slip. What do you do? You take a new grip lest you drop the item. Certainly, you remember all your years of dance instruction. You each were so good at dance, and you put in many hours of training. You know all about tired knees. Rather than just quitting, though, you do exercises to strengthen your knees. Sure, you take a quick break during practice or rest between performances, but then you jump right back in ready to go.

Much like a coach, while I was tired and down, God was exhorting me with these words. Take a new grip. Work to get stronger. The writer of Hebrews is quoting from the prophet Isaiah in chapter 35, where the prophet explains how God will bring restoration, even to the point of deserts springing into bloom with flowers. The news that God is coming, that He is restoring and changing, is the encouragement. Isaiah says, and the writer of Hebrews echoes then, "strengthen...encourage." Paul echoes this same exhortation to consistency, to not giving up in his letter to the churches in Galatia, writing at the end of that letter (6:9) "let's not get tired of doing what is good." The Greek there can be translated as "don't grow weary" or "do not become discouraged" or even "do not lose heart."

Why? Because God has His own timing, and in that timing, things will produce an outcome that He desires. That timing may not be what we want; it often is NOT what we want or would choose. The outcome may not even look like anything we would wish or claim or desire. Yet, our call as the disciple is to follow with joy in whatever path He prepares remembering that we cannot see the future like He does. In the face of the difficulty, we keep going with hope and joy.

Even better, we do this for each other. To me, what was most stirring when God presented me with this verse was this part in verse 13. After taking the new grip and getting stronger, realize that you are taking that next step not just for yourself, but instead to help mark out a straight path for others who are weaker, who might be "lame" in their steps.

That call out to "make a straight path" is quoting Proverbs 4:26, but really there are a myriad of verses that suggest this. God calls us to a straight path that He will provide. He will guide our steps along the path (remember when we looked at Proverbs 3:5-6?). He lays out the narrow way for us. That concept of a straight path is a metaphor for "God's way." Stay on God's way. And here, it's suggesting that we each help one another by marking that path. God has called the Christian into a communal relationship as I told you when we looked at the John 13 passage. The totality of the New Testament is really a handbook of how a group of believers should to live together in the world. The author of Hebrews knows that at times, each one of us will get tired or discouraged. To help, as we take that fresh grip, on strengthened knees, we are then marking the pathway for others in the group.

In my 50s as my elder years come closer, this verse continues to resonate with me. I hope you girls see it now, early in your 20s, and determine to go this way with Him.

Chapter 30

I Corinthians 1:18—The message of the cross is foolish to those who are headed for destruction! But we who are being saved know it is the very power of God.

1:25 This foolish plan of God is wiser than the wisest of human plans, and God's weakness is stronger than the greatest of human strength.

1:27a Instead, God chose things the world considers foolish in order to shame those who think they are wise.

Just on first glance, I am certain you can see a trend in these three verses. As we head toward the end of the book, this is another passage God brought to me anew in the season after Numinous ended. Part of why I have written to you is my prayer that even as the years go forward into the 21st century, if Jesus tarries in His return, that you grow deeper in your faith. There will be many continued, yet not new, attacks on the Christian faith, both corporately and individually, the insidious effort to cause you to grow cold in faith. I pray that you hold firmly to our faith.

One of the most common attacks on the Christian faith is that the entire premise is foolish. It not only can be attacked as "making no sense" but that believing in Jesus seems so idiotic. *"What, the plan is for the supposed 'son of God' to come to earth only to die? And for whom...all the losers who have no power, no money, no status...plus, most humans are broken, often evil to one another, and...well, who would create a plan to save those people?"*

This is not a new attack. Paul addressed the same tone in his first letter to the city of Corinth written around 55 AD, about 25 years after Jesus. Remember Corinth is one of the major cities in Greece, and though no longer independent (all of Greece was controlled by Rome, as was most of the "Middle East"), still an important city in the region. In Greece, the love of the mind was a central aspect of the culture. You should know of the great philosophers like Plato as well as familiar philosophies like Stoicism; the wealth of Western philosophy comes directly from Greece. Those living there had a natural pride in that mental excellence. Thus, it's not surprising that the faith was most directly criticized about its logic in a place like Corinth.

Right out of the gate in his letter, Paul answers this. If you read the first four chapters, in at least ten different verses, the apostle uses this question of wisdom and folly as a way to teach about the faith. The two, wisdom and foolishness, are of course opposites. It isn't surprising that we understand that wisdom is the better of the two options. The Bible itself presents to the reader the goal of obtaining wisdom. The entire book of Proverbs can we understood as an exhortation and guide to the life-goal of becoming wise.

Here, Paul flips it around in order to make the deeper point about God's "upside down" world. We've noted elsewhere in this writing about this. If one wishes to save their life, they have to give it away to death. If you want to be the leader, then you must serve others. If you want to be honored at the head table, in your work, in some ability you have, you should actually stay quiet about it—take a seat in the back of the room. When you give to others, say nothing about it. The peace that Jesus brings will cause division and strife because He calls us to find world-peace by stopping your personal war with God...and that faith will cause others to become frustrated with you. If you have personal wealth, give it all away.

The upside-down world sure looks foolish...and it is on this point that Paul pounces. Paul is responding to a letter that contains many issues he plans to address, which he does starting in chapter 5. But the overall tone of the comments in the letter to him is somewhat dismissive, suggesting that he may not be as smart as he is portrayed. In specific, there is some suggestion that their current spiritual leader is far wiser and savvier that Paul. The people seem to suggest that being verbally creative and witty is impressive. So, Paul addresses that issue, not to tear down the other spiritual leader, and he does so by showing the Corinthians that God's measurement of things like wisdom or power or status are very different than the world's.

The Greek word for fool is one that, when you read it, will instantly see why it captures me: moria. Yep, the same word that JRR Tolkien used as a name for one of the great mines of the Dwarf people in his Middle Earth world. Later, Tolkien was actually asked about this, and he does state in a letter that he didn't intentionally use the word, but I don't fully believe him. As a Christian and a linguist, he would know that in the Greek "moria" means foolish. He describes a location that the Dwarves will again and again foolishly pursue; this cannot be accidental.

I love the wordplay that Tolkien uses when he describes how the wizard Gandalf died in the minds of Moria. That discussion comes in the land of the elves called Lothlorien which was led by two great Elves, Celeborn and Galadrial. The Lady Galadriel was actually the stronger and wiser of the two. As they discussed what had happened, Celeborn said, "one would say that at the last Gandalf went from wisdom into folly, going needlessly into the net of Moria."

Galadriel rebukes her husband saying, "He would rash indeed that said that thing; needless were none of the deeds of Gandalf in life. Those that followed him knew not his mind and cannot report his full purpose."

You might remember that more vividly from the movie where it is one of the nine companions, Legolas the elf, who says, "For we rushed needlessly into the net of Moria." He is rebuked by Galadriel who says in the movie, ""Needless were none of the deeds of Gandalf in life." In other words, Gandalf's actions may look foolish to you now, but you can't fully understand. Sure enough, later in the story, we see that there was a larger plan at work involving Gandalf.

Paul writes much the same thing about God to the followers in Corinth. "This foolish plan of God is wiser than the wisest of human plans, and God's weakness is stronger than the greatest of human strength."

Tolkien wrote about Gandalf, "Those that followed him knew not his mind and cannot report his full purpose." Tolkien was right! We've already seen this in the letter to the Ephesian church.

His mighty power…[can] accomplish
infinitely more than we imagine

Paul goes even further saying that God's plan that looks foolish is very intentional. Why? Well, for one reason to make the point that we humans cannot understand the mind of God. For another reason, much like God did several times with the nation of Israel, He wants to make sure no human attempts to claim any of the glory, claim any of the honor of successful choices made. We humans cannot save ourselves. In fact, we will make things worse. We need saving. We need a hero to come for us.

This is Paul's emphasis in verse 23. "So when we preach that Christ was crucified, the Jews are offended and the Gentiles say it's all nonsense." I love the word for offended in the Greek: scandalon, which of course you can see this is where we get our English word "scandalous." The idea that the Son of God would die for the humans is a scandal. A "can you believe it; what an offensive act"...offensive in what happened (the crucifixion) and in what it suggests (we bear sins that must be cleansed in order to holy for a Holy God).

A scandal and moria...foolish. That is the point that Paul is making in verse 25.

This foolish plan of God is wiser than the wisest of human plans

God has a plan to save humanity, and that plan looks foolish. It's one of God's upside-down plans, not the way we'd do it. Of course, Paul wants us to understand that God's foolishness is deeper than any human wisdom. But more than that, God wants to make another point.

Not only is His mind beyond ours and not only is He taking pains to ensure none of claim the credit, He wants to emphasize that He is for everyone. In Corinth, just like our world today, everyone glorifies and magnifies the famous, the rich, and the powerful. For a variety of reasons, there will always be a tiny minority of people who seem to be great and will be further honored and glorified by us humans. If you wrote a narrative about some great power coming to a place to save some people, most would assume the famous or the rich would be who gets saved. And, whether we like to admit it or not, most of us agree with that....or at the very least, we secretly want to be one of the rich or powerful.

Oh sure, people will complain about the privileged, but typically they just want to be the rich and the powerful. Look how we follow and study those people. We are "followers" on social media. We listen avidly to TV shows or the news that report about the doings or actions of the famous.

God instead came for the rest of us, the outsiders, the nobodies. Paul lays that out wonderfully in the next three verses. He emphasizes that God chose a certain type of person. God intentionally chose the foolish (or those at least that the world considers foolish) in order to shame the wise. He chose the weak in order to shame the powerful. He chose the despised (those of "low birth"...someone like me, a descent of peasants and sharecroppers) in order to shame those of exalted or privileged birth.

On that third comparison, Paul is reflecting on the comparison of birth status, so for us we might think about the children of the famous. Think about how easy it is for the child of a famous actor to get chances to act. Or the child of a rich banker, how easy it often is for that child to get entrance to the exclusive famous University. The words Paul uses there is the equivalent of a Greek slur that would suggest such a lowly lower-class person is a "thing not being" or "things which are not." You are lowly to the point that you might as well not exist! God flips this around. He chose the people "which are not" in order to unmake what the world values, what the world sees as valuable.

God chose those not made (the lowly) in order to unmake those who think they are (the famous, the privileged)

The Greek word for God's action there is also beautiful. It is usually translated as "chose," which of course makes sense. But look deeper to see this Greek word states God "picked out for and by Himself." He didn't assign this task to another. He's not like a very busy person who has an assistant go to the store to make a purchase. No, instead with God, there is deep intentionality there. God chose you. God KNOWS you. Even though, as Paul writes, not many of us "were wise by human standards," nor "powerful" and not "born into privilege," God still chose us!

Isn't that gorgeous? And just to make sure we understand, look at the v 29; God did all of this so no one would boast, exactly like those people were boasting, and in doing so, "putting down" Paul.

As I have already referenced, I believe the country of USA is sick. We are addicted to ease and luxury. We are just like the people of Corinth. We are all rich, powerful and privileged. No one in the USA isn't, at least when I am writing that in the early 21st century. And we love to honor, to mimic, and to idolize others who we perceive to be even richer, more powerful and more famous than ourselves.

In that illness, that gluttony of excess, we can believe that we don't need God. We think we can get along fine without God. Look around and you'll see many claiming a path of salvation—sometimes through politics, sometimes through owning certain things, maybe through protests—a path of salvation that does not need God. God, though, shows His saving power by choosing INTENTIONALLY the fool, the weak and the person of no status.

Girls...regardless of what the world says about you, choose to humble yourself and realize that you were chosen by God. Others might tell Him to not pick you, that you are nobody, that you aren't worth the effort. The world would say that expending energy to save you is foolish, a waste of time.

God says the opposite. Foolish are none of the deeds of God.

Believe Him.

Chapter 31

Psalm 119:72—Your instructions are more valuable to me than millions in gold and silver.

This chapter begins the end of the book. As I told you previously, I wrote a Bible study on this Psalm back in 2015, so the ideas and concepts here are most fresh to me. I've saved this verse to the end of the book because I wanted to stress to you what hopefully is obvious about my heart in writing all of this to you. The Bible is the foundation of your faith. Thus learning it, reading it, memorizing it and meditating on it are vital to a happy, successful life.

There are, of course, many other verses in the Bible that would suggest this, but when I was completing this study on the overall Psalm, I was really captured by how many times the Psalmist made this claim. As I wrote in that Bible study on Psalm 119, when we say there is a huge, long chapter in the Bible extolling the law of God, the demand to walk in His ways, that usually will sound daunting or even unpleasant. Many people like to claim that they are a "law and order" person, but everyone I know (including me) actually enjoys having the freedom to do whatever they want. NO ONE likes being told that they can't do something, or that the thing they want to do is "bad" or "immoral" or "against the law" (human or God).

As I went deep into Psalm 119, I discovered four or five major themes in the work. This theme, though, was the one that surprised me the most. As I have already recounted when we look at the "lamp and light" verse from this chapter, I had approached this famous psalm as just a long list of God's laws. Things we should obey. That we'd BETTER obey. And, sure, that God's law was good. I knew that; I was living it out as an adult. And yet....

The suggestion of verse 72 is something different. It describes someone with a deep passion, a love affair that could lead one to a deep attraction. It presented something that I had not really thought much about regarding God's law. The Psalmist wrote of having a desire connected with joy at God's ways, God's laws. Honestly, even as I write this, I am still blown away with the passion in the words. This is not the idea of legalism or avoiding punishment. Here is zest. Here is energy. Here is enthusiasm and great enjoyment.

Once when I was in college, I had a girlfriend. I must admit that I was deeply infatuated with her, though I wasn't mature enough to understand that I wasn't anywhere close to the concept of love. In my youthful enthusiasm for her, one day while I was in a long three-hour class, we were given a 15-minute break. This happened long before the days of cell phones, so I had no way to alert her I was coming. Still, I knew she was supposed to be studying at the library, which was about a 10-minute walk away from the building where my class was. I decided that if I ran, I could make it quicker, have five extra minutes with her, and then run back in time for class. So, off I dashed. Sure enough, I found her (she was greatly surprised and happy to see me). We had our moment, and then I dashed back to class. I was a few minutes late, and fortunately for me, was in a class with my favorite professor who liked me and probably gave me more slack than I deserved.

That is what the Psalmist is writing about, a passion for God's law like a lover who would run across campus for five minutes with the beloved. A deep desire and passion for God is expressive, like the feeling between two lovers. This theme is throughout the Psalm nineteen times: 14, 16, 20, 36, 40, 47, 54, 58, 72, 77, 97, 103, 111, 127, 131, 143, 161, 162, and 174.

Yet, six of those 19 verses go even deeper into something that should surprise or challenge most Americans. As you can read, it speaks specifically about have a greater love for God's word than riches.

> *v 14: "I have rejoiced in your laws as much as in riches."*
>
> *v 36: "Give me an eagerness for your laws rather than a love for money!"*
>
> *v 72: "Your instructions are more valuable to me than millions in gold and silver."*
>
> *v 111: "Your laws are my treasure; they are my heart's delight."*
>
> *v 127: "Truly, I love your commands more than gold, even the finest gold."*
>
> *v 162: "I rejoice in Your word like one who discovers a great treasure*

Most of us can think of what we would do if we gained "millions in gold." We perhaps have a list of items or places or gifts we would purchase as soon as we got that money. Our desire for wealth (part of our national sickness that I wrote about in earlier chapters) impacts us in multiple ways. This starts when we are in school. You'll be asked "what do you want to do in life"? The thought is supposed to be aimed at what major you will study and should be connected to your personal interest. Yet, over the past 30-40 years the idea has been much more about "what job do you want in the future." And, if the job you choose isn't heading to what others perceive to be a wealth-generating type jobs, they think of you as foolish. Tragically, where one used to think of doing work for which one has an interest and can see that such a job will be a plus-benefit to society, now the focus is solely on money. I have counseled dozens, even hundreds of students who were in fields of study that they admitted were unpleasant or didn't fit them well, and yet they would not leave or try another field that did interest them solely on the basis of the future job wealth potential.

That is the epitome of finding something valuable, something you'll give your life to in order to obtain "millions in gold." The Psalmist is urging us to think of God's law that way. In those other verses, we see phrases like "my heart's delight" or "as much as in riches" or "a great treasure." What we need in our life focus is precisely that, someone who will pursue God's word with that same energy and passion.

Think about how many hours a person might put on the job? Or, someone devotes to a "side gig" that they think could really help them gain more money? The length of time someone puts into gaining new competencies or further education beyond in order to get a bump in salary? None of those things is necessarily wrong, of course, but if I put in, say, 3 extra hours a day to achieve a new job skill or start a second income, the Psalmist is suggesting such energy ought to be precisely how I approach God's law.

Why?

I mean, this is the million-dollar question, right? Hopefully you can already guess the answer by having read this far in the book.

The Bible is God's delivered directions to us, a guidebook. Of course, that story is folded into a historical review of events that occurred 2000+ years ago. Within that long narrative of a specific people, telling of God's hand on and guidance for those people, truth emerges for us in the current day that informs us.

The Bible is the foundation. You can see this through how often it is criticized by many. The attack on its veracity and historical accuracy would suggest that everyone understands that the Bible stands at the center of this faith. Since the Bible gives us a historical review of events long ago, and since it places God's active work in that story, it is fair to consider or even question the historical standing of the Bible.

I won't take too much of your time now with the full defense within Christian apologetics, but I am sure you remember that I have spent my entire adult life focused on this. Based on the historical and documentary evidence, I tell you that as a Christian theologian and as a Historian, the Bible is the most historically accurate writing in all of antiquity. The depth of this defense was understood when the various New Testament writers were crafting their letters.

Paul brings in very early evidence that he received, somewhere between 33-36 AD, a mere few years after Jesus' death and resurrection when he writes to the Christians in the Greek city of Corinth. He says, in chapter 15, starting at verse 3, "I passed on to you what was most important and what had also been passed on to me." He then describes the overall core of the Christian faith, including naming eyewitnesses (read vv 3-7). In other words, he was telling his readers that "you can go check this out," rather than suggesting "just believe me." This is astounding evidence, easily undercutting any suggestion of myth regarding the Christian story. Myth takes hundreds of years to emerge within a culture, not three or four years. Moreover, for no other historical figure or event from antiquity do we have this kind of documentary evidence in either the sheer volume of manuscripts or the few years between writing and the event itself.

Later, in that same chapter, Paul focuses their attention on this point, that this historical act did happen, and thus all of the theological position of the Christian faith hinges on this. In the middle of this description, he makes the logical point that all of their hopes and suggestions of how to live, let alone their personal suffering for their faith, was pointless and even foolish without the historical event being true. Paul says, "And if our hope in Christ is only for this life, we are more to be pitied than anyone in the world."

So, the Bible is at the core of the Christian faith. It contains for us the direction of how to live. Remember when we looked at the first verses of Psalm 1? Remember the concepts from the Proverbs 3 verses? Again and again, what I have wanted you to glean from this book is how central the Bible must be for your lives. It's not a sideline thing. It's not a book you just have around, something you maybe open once a week.

My prayer for you is that your desire for God's word does become as great as riches. Invest hours into reading this treasure, seeking deeper understanding of God's word to us. Make your passion for Him, and the fame of His name centered on the truth of His word, as the most important thing in your life. I pray that God will awaken, or keep the fire stoked high, to have a great passion, even as strong as what the Psalmist says we need—more valuable than millions in wealth.

Chapter 32

II Timothy 4:7—I have fought the good fight, I have finished the race, and I have remained faithful.

Here at the close, you probably can tell why I chose to end my writing to you with this verse. As I have tried to impress on you through the writing, the Christian experience is of a journey. In one sense, I have given you a written testimony of my own journey. Of course, life is this...a journey over years. You start out as a child, barely realizing one day becomes another. Somewhere in your latter teens, you start to think a bit about the future...what school to attend, what job to pursue, and who to marry.

As you reach your 20s, life is usually new and fresh as all the adult things come at you. First job, first house, a wedding and maybe a baby, first raise or promotion...it's all kind of exciting. And yet, as one reaches their 30s, some monotony sets in as you realize the sameness of each year. It does not have to be monotonous, and rarely is boring, but still the fact emerges that things don't seem to change. This truth begins to really reinforce the length of the life journey. As you know, I am writing this while in my later 50s, and I certainly do feel the miles, both physically and emotionally.

For the Christian, as we have seen, the image of moving on a pathway led and guarded by God is a central image. I like to think about it similarly to the video games you've seen me play where you start the game with a character, and as you move through the game, you level up. The character changes, and in some games, they do a good job of showing the weight of your choices. If you do "bad things," your character might become scarier. If you do educational things, your character becomes more wise and able to do actions connected to the mind.

Well, the Christian experience is similar. God calls us and when we respond, it's like we respawn into the game as a level 1 character. He is ready to guide us. He gives us more mature advisors. We soon find ourselves on the journey with a few friends, usually close in age, who are also learning and growing. Soon enough, if we stay focused on His path, we start to level up in the faith and how to navigate in the world. We learn to hear His voice more easily; we see the twists and turns more clearly.

Finally, though, you arrive at the end of your life. We aren't there yet, as far as we know, but that last day could come at any time. However, that's not really what this verse is truly suggesting. Yes, we want to live each day knowing that we have no control on what may transpire, and in some situations, it might indeed be our last day. Paul, writing to his younger partner Timothy, has realized that he is much older and far closer to the end, and so is urging Timothy be aware of the long journey.

Your mother and I studied Paul's second letter to Timothy together way back in the mid-90s when I was the Student Pastor at First Baptist Church in Winter Park. She had been doing Precept Ministry Bible studies a bit before I did, but the Church brought Kay Arthur's team to lead everyone in a training weekend. I loved the way they taught how to study the Word.

Of course, I had "done" Bible study through seminary, and had read this verse before, but this was an immersive study that dug deeply into what Paul was trying to communicate.

This verse has become more poignant to me as I have aged. I pray God gives me many more years; I joke that I have the blood of Númenor when people believe that I am 15-20 years younger than I truly am. You remember that I have worked out for the past 15 years in order to be as physically healthy as possible, keeping my weight down and the muscle tone intact. And yet, as 60 starts to come into view for me, I feel the years. And regardless of how much effort I might put into working out or eating well, the miles I have to go is less than when I was younger. There is less time on the game clock for me.

Paul was in prison when he wrote this letter, and it is possibly the last thing that he wrote, at least of surviving letters. While Paul could not know the future any better than us, he does seem to have a sense that his time on the journey was coming to an end. The verse immediately before this makes that clear when Paul says, "the time of my death is near."

This last section of the book is one of the most personal for Paul. All of his writings are in his voice, and you sense the man behind the pen, sharing his feelings and ideas when he writes. Yes, God is directing the words, informing the writing through the Holy Spirit, but there is always a real human involved in the Bible's various books. In many of Paul's letters, you can see a younger man trying to counsel a church or correct wrong theology. At times he is fighting back against those who lied about him or were trying to introduce error. Here, though, it's a very private letter between friends, and the intimacy is clear.

This verse comes at the very end of the letter, and you can almost sense Paul's reluctance to close the letter. This could be the last thing he says to his close friend, Timothy. In verse 9, he begs Timothy to come to him, but we don't know if Timothy ever made it to see Paul. The verses after that he goes into some memories, mentioning friends Timothy would know too and people to watch out for, who had done Paul harm. Its personal. Its visceral. So, when you read verses 1-8, you are reading the closing more formal thoughts of Paul, wishing Timothy to be as ready as possible for the years ahead after Paul is dead.

So, he then says this amazing verse of confidence to Timothy. He is aware his time is limited. He knows he may never see Timothy again. Paul knows there won't be other missionary journeys, no new church that he starts. He is poignant, but he is unbroken. Look at the words again:

> *I have fought the good fight.*
> *I have finished the race.*
> *I have remained faithful.*

In the "fought the good fight" phrase, think back to the many moments I have told you about this struggle each Christian has. We learned to put on the armor of God in Ephesians 6. I showed you that before the armor, you need the clothing of love and mercy Paul wrote about in Colossians 3. We saw in the second letter to the Corinthians that we are fighting with holy weapons, and we know from those verses, as well as II Peter, that we aren't fighting against other humans, but rather an enemy that is powerful. That enemy is dangerous, yet already defeated.

In the "finished the race" idea, remember what we saw from the prophet Habakkuk, that we are to wait patiently. Think back to the first verse I taught you, my life verse from Isaiah...we walk and do not faint. We run and don't grow weary. Isaiah reminded us also to set our face like stone, strongly determined to do His will. That same concept was expressed by the writer of Hebrews, with the exhortation to strengthen your knees to continue the journey.

In the "remained faithful" concept, go back to the verse I showed you in Paul's letter to the church at Philippi. He reminds us that with Jesus, I can do all things. I can stand and stay faithful. Regardless of the circumstances, I have never lacked because He has always been with me. In that same letter, in chapter 3, read again how Paul says that he will keep pressing on to finishing the race.

Paul brings up this idea of completing the journey and staying faithful on the path multiple times. One of my favorites is in his second letter to the church at Corinth. In that letter, he is describing how much opposition and persecution he has suffered. But look at what he writes:

> *That is why we never give up. Though our bodies are dying, our spirits are being renewed every day. For our present troubles are small and won't last very long. Yet they produce for us a glory that vastly outweighs them and will last forever! So we don't look at the troubles we can see now; rather, we fix our gaze on things that cannot be seen. For the things we see now will soon be gone, but the things we cannot see will last forever.*

I think this wonderful passage can take the word "troubles" beyond only the idea of the persecutions that we might undergo, into an even broader idea of "everyday challenges" or "experiences that frustrate us." So, we don't give up because the "everyday challenges and experiences that frustrate us" are small and won't last very long. Yet they produce for us a "weight of glory." The Greek word for weight is meant to show that the glory is heavier, or more enduring perhaps, vaster, than the troubles. So do what instead? The exact same tactic that I showed you in Chapter 25--Fix your eyes on things that cannot yet now be seen, on heavenly things. Back again we go to the war in the mind, the tension between being conformed or being transformed, and our active role in that experience. As we go along, actively submitting to God's way and actively fixing our thoughts on the truth He wants for us, on the good and the holy, we move ever confidently forward.

We never give up! Even as death comes closer, day by day, we realize any troubles or issues are small, temporary. He isn't suggesting ignoring the obvious but much like the upside-down world of God we talked about earlier in the book, Paul knows that there is far more to the world than we can see in this physical place.

Thus, we don't stare at, don't fixate on the issues, whether functional issues (like a car problem or money challenge) or personal (like aging, illness). Instead, we focus our vision, our gaze on these deeper spiritual things.

That focus, that determination is what provides Paul the ability to then say later he is ready to go home to God. He knows he has remained faithful on the journey. So, here at the end of this book, I say the same to you, my beloved daughters. I'd love to have more years if God wishes to give them to me. And yet, I am ready to go home to Him knowing that through all of the issues of my life, I have fought the good fight, have finished my race, and have kept the faith.

This is the target. You don't want any wasted years, wasted days. You want to be able to wake up each day and say a version of "if this is the last day, I am content because I have fought the good fight, have finished my race, and have kept the faith." God is not looking at what the world calls success. Remember His ways are not our ways, and though the world thinks they are foolish, instead they are the path of wisdom. He doesn't consider our bank account. He isn't counting the people you have told about Jesus or helped become saved. We saw earlier in the verses from the prophet Micah, Hosea and Zachariah what God is considering. Paul is confident not in his resume of some churches started or personal fame; rather he is confident of the crown of righteousness that will be given to Him by the righteous Judge because he, Paul, has stayed the course.

At some point, my dear daughters, I will leave you. I will be sad when that happens as you, my daughters, have given me the greatest joy in life. There is nothing else I have ever produced that remotely comes close to the pride I feel in you. You are my greatest treasure. I will not wish to leave you. And yet, when the day comes, I will say with Paul that I am ready. I already feel like my life has been poured out as an offering. I have remained faithful and will continue to do so for the days left that he gives me.

In *Fellowship of the Ring,* Frodo realizes just how big of a responsibility he now has with the powerful and awful ring. In the book, Gandalf and Frodo are talking at Bag End (in the movie, this conversation comes in the mines of Moria), and Gandalf says that the enemy has come back, mostly because of the ring. Frodo then says, "I wish it need not have happened in my time." Gandalf then replies "So do I, and so do all who live to see such times. But that is not for them to decide. All we have to decide is what to do with the time that is given us."

Whether you find yourself alive in overly perilous times or in times of plenty, in days of revolt or of societal unity, you get to decide what to do with that time. God's call to you and to me and to all who live is to live like Paul, a life of faithful endurance accomplishing daily the tasks God gives you. Those tasks may seem epic like Frodo's journey, or they may simply be the call to show grace or mercy to another, to your neighbor. You might have a massive leadership decision that will impact hundreds, maybe even thousands of employees, or you might simply have the task of remaining in humility, not thinking too highly of yourself.

In all the things you do and all the paths on which you trod, my prayer for you is that you keep God's word close to your heart. He loves you even more than I do. Those words will surely guide your steps, so lean not to your own understanding but rather on His. Give him glory and honor in each day that He gives you, determined to acknowledge Him consistently, and you can say this same confident statement with Paul, and me.

I love you,

Daddy

Appendix

The more I study, the more I fall in love with the Word. I told you in the introduction that there were far more verses to include than I did. I ended up with 31, but of course if you read carefully, you realize that at points I included a few other verses that fit well. So, here at the end, I did another pass through my many notes on various other verses to see if I should highlight others for you...and of course I found several. You'll note that I still haven't included the famous verses like John 3:16 or Matthew 28:18-20 or Romans 3:23 or a chapter like I Corinthians 13 or Psalm 23. Those, and many others, are so worthy of your study. I beg you to expend your life learning more about God's Word. Still, I wanted to share a few more verses that over the years have meant something to me. Hopefully, as you read these, you too will be encouraged.

Isaiah 55:1 -- "Is anyone thirsty? Come and drink—even if you have no money! Come, take your choice of wine or milk—it's all free!

The image of God as giver of water is important throughout the Scripture. Here the NLT is lacking a tad in that the Hebrew would add "come to the waters" at the end of verse 1. Over the years, I have noted this theme in multiple places. Jeremiah 2:10 uses this image in a judgement against us humans who seek for water elsewhere, other than God. Exodus 17 and Psalm 95:8 and also in Hebrews 3&4 we see God's complaint about how we complain, asking for water and, in essence ignore that He is the Fountain of life. Psalms 42 and 63 both talk about our need to recognize our own thirst, and then find it quenched through Him only. And Jesus declares His own divinity through this sign in John 4:13-14 and 7:37-39. Finally, though probably not exhaustively, we see how God declares the beauty and wonder and life-giving nature of the Holy City on Rev 22:1 with its river of life, and then the invitation to come and drink in 22:17.

Isaiah 43:2-- When you go through deep waters, I will be with you. When you go through rivers of difficulty, you will not drown. When you walk through the fire of oppression, you will not be burned up; the flames will not consume you.

God is faithful to be with you, again the idea of Immanuel. Note, this verse doesn't say that you won't have to go through the deep waters or the fire...just that you won't be ultimately destroyed nor be alone. Like Psalm 23, in the presence of my enemies, He prepares a what I need to survive.

Isaiah 26:3-8--You will keep in perfect peace all who trust in you, all whose thoughts are fixed on you! Trust in the Lord always, for the Lord God is the eternal Rock. He humbles the proud and brings down the arrogant city. He brings it down to the dust. The poor and oppressed trample it underfoot, and the needy walk all over it. But for those who are righteous, the way is not steep and rough. You are a God who does what is right, and you smooth out the path ahead of them. Lord, we show our trust in you by obeying your laws; our heart's desire is to glorify your name.

I was first drawn to this passage through the Passion ministry of Louie Giglio. That ministry claimed Isaiah 26:8 as their foundation verse. The words before it, claiming the promise of a God who stays with us is perhaps even more powerful. The idea of "our heart's desire" is born out of the response to whom God is. The way of peace rolls through obedience to God's ways. We don't get to have "perfect peace" simply because we wish it or because God just likes us. Instead we have a determined focus on Him and His ways, making that our heart's desire.

Joshua 14:10-12 (this is about Caleb, the other spy who went into the promised land, as told way back in Exodus)--**"Now, as you can see, the Lord has kept me alive and well as he promised for all these forty-five years since Moses made this promise—even while Israel wandered in the wilderness. Today I am eighty-five years old. I am as strong now as I was when Moses sent me on that journey, and I can still travel and fight as well as I could then. So give me the hill country that the Lord promised me. You will remember that as scouts we found the descendants of Anak living there in great, walled towns. But if the Lord is with me, I will drive them out of the land, just as the Lord said."**

The Hebrew says "as my strength was then, so is my strength now, for battle and for going out and coming in." I love that. Caleb is my current Biblical figure to model as I head towards older years...that I too would still have my strength and be using it for God and God's glory. I also love the last verse here where he states his intention, but acknowledges that the success of the venture lies with the Lord..."perhaps if God is with me..." We are told this often in the Bible...don't say I will do X or I plan to do Y...but simply say "if the Lord allows" or "not my will but Yours." We have no control over our lives, cannot extend it one breath or grow one inch...we are but a vapor, so the things we determine to do are only as God allows.

Deuteronomy 6:4-9 -- "Listen, O Israel! The Lord is our God, the Lord alone. And you must love the Lord your God with all your heart, all your soul, and all your strength. And you must commit yourselves wholeheartedly to these commands that I am giving you today. Repeat them again and again to your

children. Talk about them when you are at home and when you are on the road, when you are going to bed and when you are getting up. Tie them to your hands and wear them on your forehead as reminders. 9Write them on the doorposts of your house and on your gates.

Here is the core idea of what the human does in the relationship with God, after one comes to awakening, through Jesus. We are dead or blind or lost—usually unaware of this state—then through Jesus comes Awakening, coming alive, able to see and be found. So then what? You learn to love God wholly (v5). You learn to walk with Him in His ways (v6–9). You teach and pass them on to your children, both with verbal instruction and visible yet non-verbal reminders (v7-9). You express your devotion to Him and His ways in front of your community, at work, in the marketplace, and in your neighborhood (v8-9).

II Corinthians 1:3-4 -- All praise to God, the Father of our Lord Jesus Christ. God is our merciful Father and the source of all comfort. He comforts us in all our troubles so that we can comfort others. When they are troubled, we will be able to give them the same comfort God has given us.

Powerful idea for anyone going through challenging times. One reason we go through things, trials, afflictions is so that we can be a comfort and encouragement to others when they go through the same thing. For this to happen, it demands community and a willingness to invest in others, but also demands the courage and determination to make it through that trial when it first comes to you.

Psalms 139:6-- Such knowledge is too wonderful for me, too great for me to understand!

God is "Wholly Other." This is a key part of the numinous idea...God is beyond us. Not just smarter than us, but completely and utterly beyond us. He is a Being, but not like us, not of us. Were He not gracious, and thus willing to reveal Himself, we would remain ignorant of Him. Yet, He is gracious, and thus through creation, through His word, and through His coming to us, Immanuel, He has revealed himself. But, take care as many confuse this fact to mean that they know God and/or know all about God. There is no possibility that a human does either....we know, rather, what He has chosen to reveal. At the top of our knowing ability, there is still more of God, far beyond our capability.

Proverbs 1:7-- Fear of the Lord is the foundation of true knowledge, but fools despise wisdom and discipline.

In many respects, the loss of this truth within the USA, within the West, is the core reason for our decline, drift and decay as a people, as a culture. Because we no longer believe in anything more than ourselves as individuals, we no longer admit there must be something beyond ourselves. In our conclusion that we are alone in the universe, we have drifted to the arrogance of thinking we are self-created, and thus in no need to discover if there is a Creator. When we turn back to this question with true humility—"I am not contingent; I was created and thus am curious to discover what or whom created me...and if that Creator requires anything from me." Then we come back to this verse in Proverbs to inquire about wisdom, to seek for understanding....and then we find ourselves like the Israelites with Moses, to our shock, seeing the awesomeness of the Being of Creation...and falling down in awe and fear at His power. Then we can say "what must I do"...and we could see our culture begin to turn again to a pursuit of virtue and right living.

Philippians 4:6-- Don't worry about anything; instead, pray about everything. Tell God what you need, and thank him for all he has done.

The closing section of Philippians, vv. 4-9, remains a clear, distinct list of "how to live as a Christian." The Bible, of course, provides several short sections like this to guide us, but here Paul runs the gamut of things to do, to focus on, and attitude issues. But this verse, which I recently studied again, just keep smacking me in the face with the reality that I am weak here. I am often anxious, about many things...so, even though I've highlighted this before, I'm doing it again as yet another call to action. I think the end phrase of v5 plays a role here...seeing that "The Lord is near!" And as He is near, He is open to hearing about the things we are concerned about. Note He doesn't say you can't think about these things...you obviously think about them if you are telling the request to Him. But I have to then relax enough to realize that in telling Him, He is near, heard and will walk with me through whatever is causing me to be anxious, causing me to dwell on it.

Matthew 6:22-23-- "Your eye is like a lamp that provides light for your body. When your eye is healthy, your whole body is filled with light. But when your eye is unhealthy, your whole body is filled with darkness. And if the light you think you have is actually darkness, how deep that darkness is!"

"And if the light you think you have is actually darkness...." Now that's a scary thought right there. Jesus comes back to this idea next chapter, Matt 7:21-23, when He tells how there will be people at the judgment who assume they are going to heaven. In other words, they don't know that what they think is the light, salvation and connection to Jesus, is actually darkness. Paul speaks of this same idea of being blind to one's own situation in I Cor 2 and II Cor 3 when he starts talking about how the old covenant is like a veil. In 3:16 he writes "whenever someone turns to the Lord, the veil is taken away." He goes on in chapter

4 to then say "Satan, who is the god of this world, has blinded the minds of those who don't believe." Still, Jesus' words in Matthew are chilling because He is talking about someone who can't see that what they think is faith, is Christianity, actually is not. They are not on the narrow road to life but on the broad road to destruction. I think the only plan to confront this blindness starts with Psalm 1:1-3...a person who has "delight in the Law of the LORD, meditating on it day and night." Stay deep in God's ways, holding that awe and reverent fear (the numinous) that without God removing the veil, we too might be blinded thinking we are good.

I John 1:9—But if we confess our sins to him, he is faithful and just to forgive us our sins and to cleanse us from all wickedness.

When we want to experience wholeness, freedom, and cleansing...move to confession. For most, we simply resist having to admit that we, too, have something to confess. We often think about that deeply in past tense. I suggest that Jesus' model prayer that highlights the request for forgiveness is a hint that daily we miss the mark of holiness, and thus have something to confess.

Hebrews 4:12--For the word of God is alive and powerful. It is sharper than the sharpest two-edged sword, cutting between soul and spirit, between joint and marrow. It exposes our innermost thoughts and desires.

This is usually the go-to verse to demonstrate why the Bible is vital in the growth of the Christian. God uses the Bible has the container, so to speak, of His revealed word for us. It is His guidebook. The Bible contains truth and direction for us on the journey, and it both guides us and reveals us.

Galatians 6:9--So let's not get tired of doing what is good. At just the right time we will reap a harvest of blessing if we don't give up.

If you think hard, you should remember me quoting this verse often, though usually with the King James Version: don't grow "weary in well-doing." As I have noted many times, the path of the Christian is challenging. It is, then, easy to get tired of always being the one to do well, to give to others, to serve, to be nice in the face of evil. On and on, the experiences can grow where you do what is right, and yet feel as if there is no payoff. Well, of course, we don't do what God asks of us because of a reward; we do good because He calls us to that life. In the face of being tired of "being the only one," keep this verse firmly in mind. Don't grow weary...keep doing it because He calls us onward.

Matthew 10:16--"I am sending you out like sheep surrounded by wolves, so be wise as serpents and innocent as doves."

This verse might actually rank in my top five most stated to young Christians as they enter the work world. I think it's might be one of Jesus's most wise statements about how to live. This idea ties directly into the verses about spiritual warfare, that there is an enemy who seeks to do hard to God's world (including you sometimes). It is not a world of peace nor is it a world of fairness. It is a tough place. So, we have His wisdom of how to go forth: wise AND innocent. The Greek here could also be understood as crafty AND harmless. Either way, the illustration is clear. The snake is not actually aggressive like a predator, but rather one that has to move stealthily through its environment. It is careful in every movement, often keep quiet as it navigates the surroundings. Meanwhile, the dove is a bird that does not hunt others nor seek to do harm. There is a reason that the dove has been a symbol of peace for many peoples and cultures. So, like the snake and the dove, we must operate in a world that will hurt us if we are unwise.

Colossians 3:17--And whatever you do or say, do it as a representative of the Lord Jesus, giving thanks through him to God the Father.

I keep several verses in my office at the College. They are almost all designed to be reminders to me, rather than verses for my colleagues or students to see. If we think that our lives are on mission (II Corinthians 5, Matthew 5), then when we have a "normal" job we might end up feeling like the work has no purpose. We can actually divert ourselves from the necessary work of that field, believing that we should go do some sort of Christian activity. Well, this verse and a few others like I Corinthians 10:31 and 15:58 remind us that we really work for God. We should think of our bosses and supervisors as not truly being the boss, but God Himself. Do all of our work as His representative, doing our very best work at the task of that job.

Numbers 23:19--God is not a man, so he does not lie. He is not human, so he does not change his mind. Has he ever spoken and failed to act? Has he ever promised and not carried it through?

The theology of Numinous as it related to God is centered in the idea C.S. Lewis emphasized, that God is not one of us. Or, as Karl Barth wrote, God is the Wholly-Other. He is other than us, other than human. This verse clearly emphasizes this truth. It is vital that we hold onto this idea, especially when we feel ready to confront God on some supposed failure of His. But even better, the verse emphasizes the positive of this when it points out that unlike other humans, God does not make a promise only to bail on it. He does not fail to act after having given the assurance of doing so.

Romans 5:3-5--We can rejoice, too, when we run into problems and trials, for we know that they help us develop endurance. And endurance develops strength of character, and character strengthens our confident hope of salvation. And this hope will not lead to disappointment. For we know how dearly God loves us, because he has given us the Holy Spirit to fill our hearts with his love.

If we think the challenges of our life is pointless, these verses remind us that such is not true. Every problem, every trial is useful. Here, Paul points out that God uses these moments like a coach uses drills in workouts. They are designed to strengthen us. Peter shares a similar sentiment in II Peter 1:5-9. Peter even goes a bit further, stating that the person who does NOT grow stronger, who "does not develop in this way" will grow weaker, blind, and forgetful. Notice also that Paul links these events, something we would typically suggest as "bad" or "unfortunate to experience" as rather events that strengthen hope. And, a hope that does not disappoint!

Ephesians 4:1-3--Therefore I, a prisoner for serving the Lord, beg you to lead a life worthy of your calling, for you have been called by God. Always be humble and gentle. Be patient with each other, making allowance for each other's faults because of your love. Make every effort to keep yourselves united in the Spirit, binding yourselves together with peace.

I've said before the Ephesians is similar to a "Christianity 101" textbook. The first three chapters lay out a theology of God and His mysterious work to bring salvation to all humans. The last three chapters lay out a functional theology of how to "do church," the corporate connection of any human who has chosen to accept God's offer of salvation. He closes chapter 3 with a beautiful prayer; he opens chapter 4 with this thundering statement of what a Christian life should look like. This same sentiment is throughout the New Testament, so it doesn't have to stand alone. But my goodness, if these three verses were all we had about what a life in a passionate pursuit of God's holiness is, this would be enough. Strive to honor God, living worthy of His calling. Be humble. Be gentle. Be patient. Be forgiving. Be loving. Be united. Be one with the Holy Spirit. Be graceful. Wow!

Colossians 1:21 --This includes you who were once far away from God. You were his enemies, separated from him by your evil thoughts and actions.

This verse shocks many. I know of no one who admits they are somehow God's enemy. And I'm thinking about only my non-Christian friends, especially those who claim either to be agnostic or atheist. Even those who claim there is no God (the atheists) will say some version of "even if there was, I've never been at war with God." So, to many, the idea that their life is somehow an affront to God, somehow at enmity shocks them. Yet, God draws out the clear logical conclusion of what the fall of the human with Adam and Eve left us with. By choosing to strive for equality with God by eating the fruit of the Tree of the Knowledge of Good and Evil, we stepped into conflict with God. The entire story of the Bible then is a beautiful rescue tale of the great King coming to save us even though we were the ones who chose to walk into strife with Him. He rescues us anyway. Paul explains this same idea in Romans 5:6-11 (see especially verse 10) and Ephesians 2:4-10 (see especially verse 5). John covers similar ground in I John 4:9-16. To me, the saddest sentence is the first one... "who were once far away from God." This idea of separation hints back to the Garden were, in Genesis 3:23-24, Adam and Eve are banished from the Garden, sent far away. We've been on a quest to return ever since, and here we see that the great King has given us a way home.

About the Author

Carl Creasman has been speaking professionally for over 35 years to a wide variety of audiences here in the United States and abroad in such diverse places as Haiti and England. A gifted communicator, one College President stated, "Carl has a gift for making complex ideas easily understood," reaching audiences "with a style and message that transcends the cultural challenges of postmodernism." A speaker for numerous colleges, churches and professional organizations, he urges his listeners to achieve excellence in their personal, educational, and professional lives.

Carl began speaking during college at Auburn University, and continued to do so while earning first his Master's of History followed by a Master's of Divinity. Throughout his adult life, Carl has combined his ability as a communicator with his love of working with people. He has worked in diverse arenas such as coaching an Olympic training swim team, working construction for a custom homebuilder and ministering as the Student Pastor of a local church.

Currently a Professor of History at Valencia College in Orlando, FL, he is known for his inspiring presentations and his concern for his students. At Valencia, his student reviews tell a consistent story of value as reflected by a common statement—"you are one of the best teachers I have ever had; thank you for changing my life."

Carl is married to Kim, recently celebrating 31 years of bliss together. They have three lovely daughters, Logan, Meryn and Brynn. Since 1993, they have lived in Winter Park, FL, moving from Wake Forest, NC where Carl completed his seminary degree.

As a Professor, Minister and Speaker, Carl mixes history and spiritual depth with motivational, value-laden stories to drive home a passionate message that will leave your participants "inspired, encouraged and ready to charge forward into life." Or, as one recent participant stated, "Your words have inspired me to take a deep leap of faith and change my young life for the better."

"Carl Creasman will bring a word and story to students that will ring with authenticity . . .and plant seeds of transformation in their thinking.
Ken Dillard, University of Cincinnati, Campus Pastor Collegiate Ministry

"Carl Creasman is an innovative speaker. Students relate well to the ideas, presentation, and realization of all that Carl offers."
Amy Boyer, College of Holy Cross

"Your presentation on 'Extreme Living Extreme Valor' drove home a message that was critical to the times we are living in. As you spoke to the audience about integrity, honor, & honesty, you could feel the emotion in the crowd as they took it in."
Michael Cowles, SkillsUSA Ohio Director

"Your words were inspirational, humorous and timely."
Dr. James T. King, Vice Chancellor Tennessee Board of Regents

"Carl has been instrumental in discipling me and challenging me....He will not back down from a challenge to his faith and is open and up-front about what Christ did for him."
Rev. Kyle Gatlin, Covenant United Methodist Church, Dothan, AL

"You have a special talent to inspire, motivate and excite others toward being the very best they can be."
Dr. Kermit Carter, Dean for Student Affairs, Calhoun Community College, Decatur, AL

"Carl has a unique way to speak the truth in a way that communicates to a 21st century audience."
E. Bailey Marks, Campus Crusade for Christ, Leader-Led Movements

"Carl's ability to relate to students and professionals alike makes his work extremely relevant to both audiences."
Victor Felts, South-Eastern IFC Executive Director

"Carl's passion for God and zeal for life continue to inspire me. His trust in God in all circumstances is a continual reminder to me of God's faithfulness."
Scott Allen, Former National Collegiate Ministry, Belmont College

To invite Carl Creasman to speak at your school, conference, or church, contact:
Carl E. Creasman, Jr.
321.245.6882 or creasman@mac.com

www.carlcreasman.com

www.ingramcontent.com/pod-product-compliance
Lightning Source LLC
Chambersburg PA
CBHW022005090426
42741CB00007B/894